RUNNING TO WIN

GALENA R. CONATSER

Running To Win
by Galena R. Conatser

Printed in the United States of America

ISBN 1-594678-80-4

Unless otherwise indicated, Bible quotations are taken from the King James Version of the Bible. Scripture quotations marked AMP are taken from the Amplified® Bible, Copyright © 1954, 1958, 1962, 1964, 1965, 1987 by The Lockman Foundation.

www.xulonpress.com

ACKNOWLEDGEMENTS

Bishop and Pastor Gael Wallace – Thanks for preaching destiny messages that have changed my life. I could not have communicated my thoughts effectively in this book without quoting a few "Bishopisms." I appreciate you believing in me and encouraging me to write. I pray this project is a reflection of your influence on my spiritual growth.

Courtney Deane – Thanks for you honest opinions, suggestions, and all the hours of editing efforts. God bless you for your diligence and for your spirit of excellence.

Detroit World Outreach Pastoral Staff – Thanks for your sincere friendship and constant encouragement. I'm blessed to work with such anointed men and women of God.

International Impact Ministries Leadership – You are all so invaluable to me. Thanks for fueling this vision with your prayers and words of encouragement.

Minister Deborah Plummer – Thanks a million for being a

true friend and for the countless occasions when you simply said, "It's time." You may never know just what that meant to me.

My beautiful daughters – Thanks girls, for patiently allowing me to be the minister God has called me to be. Even as children, there's always been a special grace upon you for the works of the ministry. You are all vessels unto honor. I am proud of all of you.

My husband, Michael – Thanks, Babe. Through it all, you've always been the one to provoke me the most to pursue my God-given dreams to make a difference. God has used you in my life to convince me that I was born to win. I'm so thankful that I'm winning this race with you at my side. I love you with all my heart!

CONTENTS

FOREWORD

There are certain events in a woman's life that are antici-
pated with great expectation: high school graduation,
her wedding (the day every little girl dreams of), and the
expectation of her first child. When they finally happen,
she's usually filled with indescribable joy.

The Bible says there's an appointed time for everything.
When something is scheduled, but never takes place, it
leaves a void in a person's heart. Yet other events may take
place too soon. These experiences can result in a lost sense
of potential and purpose. Before you know it, all sense of
destiny is lost. I used to be such a woman. I've often thought
I've lived my whole life ten years ahead of schedule.

When I was very young, I spent a great deal of time with
my grandmother, Laura Sue Thacker Slone, whom I proudly
called "Granny." My mother was a working mom. She
cooked many meals, kept a neat home, and would occasion-
ally even find the time to sew. She did the very best she
could, especially considering the challenges of her day. She
would often say, "You do what you have to do" – a word of
advice I have never forgotten. My mother was and still is
wonderful, however it was my granny who had made the
greater impression upon my life. I simply adored this

woman. She seemed to always have the right answers, the right touch, and the right recipe for everything. I believed that there was nothing she couldn't do. In turn, she made me believe there was nothing that *I* could not do. She was the one who made me see redeemable value, even in my mistakes. She was a teacher in the 1930's, the kind that taught six grades in one classroom. No wonder she had such patience. Because I admired her so, I decided very early that I would also be a teacher.

As a child, I would spend hours on end pretending to be a schoolteacher. Later, I would spend much of my quiet time writing my thoughts and simple poetry. I can remember having such a strong sense of destiny as I looked forward to what I believed I would become.

But "life happens," and not always as a person plans. A few mistakes were made with my high school sweetheart, and well, we were on our way to building a life together. We seemed to be the absolute exception to what everyone said would happen to our untimely union. We actually defied the statistics on teenage marriage.

Having dedicated our lives to the Lord early in our marriage, we always endeavored to acknowledge and honor Him in bringing up our four daughters. Needless to say, we had some rough waters to cross, but love was the bridge that always built a way. My husband and I are pleased with our accomplishments, as well as forgiving of our failures. Still, for many years, there was something inside me saying that I wasn't smart because I didn't possess a diploma, that I wasn't complete because I didn't have the big wedding day with the white gown, and that my oldest children were really short-changed because their mother was too young and inexperienced.

My husband has shown himself to be an excellent provider, as well as my very best buddy. He has always encouraged me and tried to make me feel good about myself. And even through some painful parenting times, I feel my experience as a mother has been fulfilling. Yet in spite of all this, I still spent years feeling like a loser. Even as a minister, there were many times I felt inferior to others. The Bible says that it is God Who works in you to will and to do His good pleasure. Over time, prayer, study, and meditation, the Lord has worked in me "to will" – to want to be a winner regardless of past pain and disappointments. He has also worked in me a determination to do His good pleasure. Teaching God's Word has now become one of life's greatest joys. I have also determined to publish the words the Author (Jesus) has put into my heart.

Just as He has done for me, God can turn things around for you. He wants to turn your mistakes into miracles. He's even able to resurrect the dreams you thought were dead. Remember, "Life happens." Regardless of what may have happened in your past, you've been created to win.

Today's the day to accept the call. You've been chosen to run. Will you rise to the occasion and run with the full intention to win?

RUNNING TO WIN

I'm running to win,
Regardless of what others might say.
I'll not fear their rejection -
God's given me an everlasting name.

He's brought me up higher and given me joy
In His house of prayer.
He's established His altars
And is faithful to meet me there.

I'm running to win,
Regardless of how my adversary may roar.
He is made a powerless lion,
As I declare the Word of the Lord.

He may afflict me, oppose me,
He may come with his lies.
Has he forgotten my Father's ear is open,
And He hears my every cry?

God is for me, not against me.
On His Word I will stand.
It's in His strength that I run,
And I am possessing the land.

I've been promised an inheritance,
I'm a joint-heir with Him.
I've been guaranteed victory,
I can do nothing but win!

Regardless of setbacks
The Lord again will appear,
To encourage and strengthen,
And say that He is near.

I will be fruitful and multiply,
And my seed shall be great.
He will establish His covenant
As I trust in Him and wait.

There's an appointed time for the promise,
And it will be fulfilled.
What matters most
Is that I run with patience, and yield.

I'll yield to the One
Who's called me to run.
I've purposed in my heart
To glorify the Son.

So regardless of what others may say,
Regardless of what the enemy might bring my way,
Regardless of setbacks through failures or sin,
I've been chosen to run, and I'm running to win!

I'm running to win,
Regardless of what others might say.
I'll not fear their rejection -
God's given me an everlasting name.

1 RUNNING WITHOUT REJECTION

*THEREFORE THEN, since we are surrounded by
so great a cloud of witnesses [who have borne testi-
mony to the Truth], let us strip off and throw aside
every encumbrance (unnecessary weight) and that
sin which so readily (deftly and cleverly) clings to
and entangles us, and let us run with patient
endurance and steady and active persistence the
appointed course of the race that is set before us,
Looking away [from all that will distract] to Jesus,
Who is the Leader and the Source of our faith
[giving the first incentive for our belief] and is also
its Finisher [bringing it to maturity and perfection].
He, for the joy [of obtaining the prize] that was set
before Him, endured the cross, despising and ignor-
ing the shame, and is now seated at the right hand
of the throne of God.*
– Hebrews 12:1-2 (AMP)

It seems that when a person sets out to do something great
for God, they may begin with an excitement and zeal, but
it won't be long until they discover that the whole world
isn't quite as excited about their endeavor as they are. The
world won't share in their anticipation for success, in fact
they will reject it. They'll not only reject the idea, but the
person altogether. It is human nature to be envious and jealous of someone who is "going for the gold," or someone
who has the blessing of the Lord upon their lives.

You see, whether you have begun the journey or not, we

all have within us a desire for success. There is, however, a process. It does not come instantly. It is a joyful journey, but it is also a pathway of persistence, that leads to ultimate victory.

The Bible says that the soul of a sluggard desires, yet has nothing (Proverbs 13:4). The definition of a sluggard is a slothful, sluggish, lazy person. So, you can expect the slothful, lazy person to be irritated with your determination to win.

The way of the sluggard is overgrown with thorns [it pricks, lacerates, and entangles him], but the way of the righteous is plain and raised like a highway.
– Proverbs 15:19 (AMP)

We are all surrounded by people who are full of desire, but if those individuals are sluggards, they will never have their desires fulfilled. To the slothful person, it is frustrating to see a believer reaching for something that will bring honor to God and themselves.

We also have an enemy, who of course is the devil. He seeks to devour us. Many times his devouring work is slow and subtle. One of the enemy's most strategic tools against us is rejection.

Rejection comes in many forms, but you can be sure, no matter who you are, you will feel the pain of rejection in your life. For some, rejection is so deeply rooted within, that there is simply no faith left to believe that God has appointed them to excel. Many will even go as far as to say that God doesn't want to bless them with any tangible success. Nothing is further from the truth.

This message is for those who want to win; for those who want the weight of rejection lifted off of their lives. Our illustration is that of a runner. Of course we are not all runners in the athletic sense, but we each have a race set before us. Our determination to run can be deeply effected by rejection, however our attitude should be that we are going to win regardless. The question is not, "What will I do if I ever experience rejection?" Rather, the question is, "What will I do *when* I am rejected?" Will I allow rejection to take root and keep me from running to win?

You are justified in eliminating anything which hinders your drive for success, limits your ambition, or keeps you from doing what you know you should. Rejection has been used to hinder your success in life, and to keep you in a box of limitation. Remember – God has called you to lay aside every weight, and to lift all the limits off of your life.

THE CRIPPLING EFFECTS OF A CRUSHED SPIRIT

The spirit of a man will sustain his infirmity;
but a wounded spirit who can bear?
– Proverbs 18:14 (KJV)

The root of rejection can manifest itself in various forms, such as substance abuse, broken relationships, rebellion, and depression, just to name a few. As a result, many will experience divorce, poverty, child abuse, abandonment, humiliation, unwanted pregnancies, failure at school, work, etc. Rejection can take root through the repeated negative words of parents, peers, or employers; those whom we feel should accept and encourage us. Regardless of who spoke these words and caused us to experience their rejection, we must realize that it can have a crippling effect upon our lives.

If rejection has wounded your spirit, and life seems unbearable, the thought of running a race of any kind may seem overwhelming. You must let the Spirit of God reason with you. Receive the spirit of His counsel. Let that which is emotionally lame begin to heal, so you can run the race that has been set before you.

THE FRUIT OF REJECTION

*When He saw the throngs, He was moved with pity and
sympathy for them, because they were bewildered (harassed
and distressed and dejected and helpless),
like sheep without a shepherd.*
– Matthew 9:36 (AMP)

The devil knows that God wants to use your life. He is
actually terrified of what you will become in Christ, so he
begins to work against you early. The fruit of rejection may
lead to a lost sense of direction in your life. If this describes
you, remember these words: The Shepherd is still moved
with compassion when you have no sense of direction. You
are the object of His affection!

The Greek word for compassion means: a forceful,
physical reaction in a person's abdominal area. It is a reaction that demands a response. A person who is moved with
compassion cannot stand by and do nothing. Jesus is moved
with compassion for you! He is the Good Shepherd Who is
longing to lead you through the race.

Remember the man who journeyed from Jerusalem to
Jericho? He had an awful encounter with some thieves who
stripped him, wounded him, and left him to die. There was a
certain Samaritan who came along the way and had
compassion on the wounded man. The Samaritan saw to it
that he was properly cared for, even at his own expense.

Perhaps you have had similar encounters with the thief
(the devil), who has stripped you of your God-given identity, which is that of a winner. Has he wounded you again
and again through rejection? Have you ever just felt like
giving up on life? Inside you know that Jesus came to give
you abundant life, yet you are barely existing. Perhaps it
seems like *you've* been left to die. Do not despair, for Christ
is still the One Who is moved today. He is actively operating

on your behalf, even right now. Through His heartfelt compassion, He will see to it that those who are weary receive strength. If you are fearful, His perfect love can literally remove that fear. If you are perplexed and anxious, He will give you His perfect peace. If you are weighed down by what others have said about you, know that God will empower you today to lay aside every weight (every experience that left you with a wound of rejection). He will enable you to overcome anything that has slowed you down and everything that has gotten in your way.

THREE REACTIONS TO REJECTION

To lay the ax to the root of rejection, we must first identify our reactions.

Reaction #1 - Settling For Suffering

Rejection can cause people to suffer silently. They don't want to make any noise about it, so they settle for less than God's best. Their attitude is that life is too much to bear, and the weight is just *too* heavy. Those who settle for this suffering leave the door open for more rejection because they don't make good company. Others find it difficult to be around them.

This prepares the way for loneliness. He tells us that two are better than one and that it is not good for us to be alone. Why is this? Because loneliness progresses into self-pity. A person stuck in self-pity is holding onto a victim's mentality. The word victim means: to be killed, sacrificed, or destroyed. This tells me that none of us should ever see ourselves as victims. The following scripture reinforces this point:

> *We are troubled on every side, yet not distressed; we are perplexed, but not in despair; Persecuted, but not forsaken; cast down, but not destroyed;*

*Always bearing about in the body the dying of the
Lord Jesus, that the life also of Jesus might be made
manifest in our body. For we which live are always
delivered unto death for Jesus' sake, that the life
also of Jesus might be made manifest
in our mortal flesh.*
– II Corinthians 4:8-11 (KJV)

As long as we hold onto the victim mentality, we will
never truly obtain our greatness in Christ. Many times when
we look at men and women of greatness, we think that they
have never been through anything. But anyone who is walking in their God-given destiny has, at one time or another,
been hard-pressed, perplexed, persecuted, and struck down.
The Bible says that many are the afflictions of the righteous,
but He delivers us from them all (Psalm 34:19). The only
difference between someone who is great and someone who
has yet to walk in their greatness, is their ability to see themselves as the victor instead of the victim. No matter what we
face, we must remember that we are not crushed. We have
not been forsaken or destroyed.

Reaction #2 - Superficial Strongholds
Those who have superficial strongholds appear to be
happy, as though nothing bad has *ever* happened to them.
The word superficial means apparent, but not real. It also
means lack of depth. Many believers are not able to run
effectively because of wounds of rejection. They spend all
of their energy on pretending instead of running. They
simply do not want anyone to perceive what is really
beneath the surface of their "happy" faces. They are also
very lonely individuals. They will express their self-pity in
secret, but in public they will play a never-ending game of
make believe. In general, people are not comfortable around
pretenders. Nobody likes to be around a "phony."

Reaction #3 - Foolish Fighting

This person despises everything about life. They never have a real sense of satisfaction. They have no joy, and will always find something wrong with everyone and everything. Their reaction to rejection is resentment. To be resentful means to be bitter, envious, jealous, and annoyed. It was said earlier that when you set out to do something great for God, there will be some who will reject you for it. Those who reject you and your godly ambitions may be held by resentment themselves. They cannot stand to see anything good happen for anybody else. You might as well expect them to be envious and annoyed with you. It is actually their reaction to their *own* wound of rejection. This person is dealing with hatred, which leads to acts of rebellion. Unfortunately, foolish fighters may never know the joy of winning.

THE FRUIT OF ACCEPTANCE

To the praise of the glory of his grace, wherein he hath
made us accepted in the beloved.
– Ephesians 1:6 (KJV)

God's provision for rejection was Jesus. The root of rejection resulted in sinful behavior, but consider what I call "the great exchange." It happened on the cross of Christ. He took the curse so we could have His blessing (Galatians 3:13-14). He took our sin so we could have His righteousness. He took our poverty so we could enjoy His wealth (2 Corinthians 8:9). He took our death so we could have abundant life (Hebrews 2:9). He also took our rejection so that we could experience His acceptance.

The remedy for your rejection is in knowing that He has made you accepted in the beloved, the family of God. There is no greater family we can be a part of. When you are aware of His acceptance, you will not have to look for man's approval or applause. It's enough to know that the great cloud of witnesses are cheering you on, even now. Those who are aware of His acceptance have an ear to hear heaven's applause.

WHEN THEIR WORDS WOUND YOU

There is no fear in love [dread does not exist], but full-grown (complete, perfect) love turns fear out of doors and expels every trace of terror! For fear brings with it the thought of punishment, and [so] he who is afraid has not reached the full maturity of love [is not yet grown into love's complete perfection]. We love Him, because He first loved us.
– I John 4:18-19 (AMP)

The King James Version of the Bible says that fear has torment. I believe every sinful, evil thing is somehow connected to fear. Everyone who begins a race enters with the intent to win. But if the runner is tormented with the thought of losing, he will eventually give up. He may still run, but he will have resigned himself to losing anyway. This runner just endures the rest of the race. Our Christian experience is not to be endured, but to be *enjoyed*. God wants us to run with the joy of knowing we're predestined to win. Many times the joy of the journey is depleted when we encounter some type of rejection.

Here are the remedies for rejection:

Remedy #1 – Identify the source of pain, then apply the Word
For every lie, you ought to be able to quote at least one word of truth from Scripture. Prepare yourself ahead of time for the opposition. You know the patterns of your life and

those around you. Identify every lie and reverse the curse with the truth of God's Word. Truth has the power to render every lie ineffective. Begin to renew your mind with the Word of God, which is your greatest source of truth, so you can see a transformation in your life.

Remedy #2 – Keep forgiving

> *Great peace have they who love Your law; nothing shall offend them or make them stumble.*
> *- Psalm 119:165 (AMP)*

Offenses will come, but you don't have to *take* them. An offense is a cause of transgression or wrong. We've all been wronged, but we must learn to forgive, because unforgiveness is a barrier to abundance. Your race will require you to have abundance, but the weight of unforgiveness is too heavy for any believer, and it will leave you depleted. Don't ever deceive yourself by saying that you can't forgive. Jesus empowered you to forgive when He forgave all of *your* sins. The above scripture tells us that they who love God's Word will have peace. When you allow the peace derived from God's Word to rule in your heart and mind, you will not be so easily offended.

Remedy #3 – Lay down the destructive fruits of rejection

> *Wherefore seeing we also are compassed about with so great a cloud of witnesses, let us lay aside every weight, and the sin which doth so easily beset us, and let us run with patience the race that is set before us*
> *– Hebrews 12:1 (KJV)*

Resentment, bitterness, hatred, and rebellion are luxuries

you cannot afford. Study and practice the fruit of the Spirit found in Galatians 5:22-23, *"But the fruit of the Spirit is love, joy, peace, longsuffering, gentleness, goodness, faith, Meekness, temperance: against such there is no law."*

The fruit of the Spirit is God's remedy for the works of the flesh. Become spiritually-minded. It's your key to life and peace.

For to be carnally minded is death; but to be spiritually minded is life and peace.
- Romans 8:6 (KJV)

Remedy #4 – Shaking the "victim mentality"

Shake yourself from the dust; arise, sit [erect in a dignified place], O Jerusalem; loose yourself from the bonds of your neck, O captive Daughter of Zion.
- Isaiah 52:2 (AMP)

If you are bound by self-pity, you can find your freedom by shaking the victim mentality. You must stop rehearsing the situations and pain that came out of rejection. To stay in self-pity is like making a daily decision to stay in the dust. The above scripture tells us to shake ourselves from the dust and arise. We must rise out of self-pity before we can visualize ourselves as winners.

Remedy #5 - Accept His love and accept yourself
You might not like everything about your body. Who does? Your mind and emotions might cause you a lot of grief. But your spirit man is the one facet that will surpass even your criticism. You are an awesome spirit being made in the image of God. In fact, if you are born again, you are holy and righteous, just like God.

*And that ye put on the new man, which after God is
created in righteousness and true holiness.*
- Ephesians 4:24 (KJV)

If you're like me, you're looking to change a lot of
things about your life. But there are some things that need
no changing, like your God-given identity and destiny. The
path He has set you on, the gifts and callings, and every
good and perfect gift that He has given, are a result of His
love. Therefore, the perfect response to rejection is this: I've
been <u>accepted</u> in the beloved, I've been <u>anointed</u> to run, and
I'm <u>appointed</u> to win.

Enjoy the fruit of His acceptance and receive His divine
direction for the race that is set before you.

He's brought me up higher and given me joy
In His house of prayer.
He's established His altars
And is faithful to meet me there.

2 WINNING IN THE PLACE OF PRAYER

You have said, Seek My face [inquire for and
require My presence as your vital need]. My heart
says to You, Your face (Your presence), Lord, will I
seek, inquire for, and require [of necessity and on
the authority of Your Word].
– Psalm 27:8 (AMP)

Now that we have laid aside the weight of rejection, we need to enjoy His acceptance. The greatest place to experience His acceptance is in the place of prayer. It was E.M. Bounds who said that prayer is the privilege of every believer. It's unfortunate, but many believers neglect this great opportunity.

Who shall go up into the mountain of the Lord? Or
who shall stand in His Holy Place? He who has
clean hands and a pure heart, who has not lifted
himself up to falsehood or to what is false, nor
sworn deceitfully. He shall receive blessing from the
Lord and righteousness from the
God of his salvation.
– Psalm 24:3-5 (AMP)

If we would only be fully persuaded of the power of the cross, when it comes to prayer. The Bible tells us that when Jesus died, the veil separating man from God was torn. The blood of Jesus has given us free access to the throne of God.

For he is our peace, who hath made both one,
and hath broken down the middle wall
of partition between us;
- Ephesians 2:14 (KJV)

His blood has washed our hands and purified our hearts. We are fit to stand in His holy place, the place of sweet communion with our Creator. What a joy it is to know the price was paid, that we might enter into the very Presence of the Most High God.

I believe that the hand of God is stretched out toward us every day. He's constantly inviting us to come up higher to enjoy fellowship with Him. Believers who dare to go into their day without the awareness of God's Presence are like runners who attempt to run without fueling their bodies with the proper nutrients.

ONE THING IS NEEDED

One thing have I asked of the Lord, that will I seek,
inquire for, and [insistently] require: that I may
dwell in the house of the Lord [in His presence] all
the days of my life, to behold and gaze upon the
beauty [the sweet attractiveness and the delightful
loveliness] of the Lord and to meditate, consider,
and inquire in His temple. For in the day of trouble
He will hide me in His shelter; in the secret place of
His tent will He hide me; He will set me high upon a
rock. And now shall my head be lifted up above my
enemies round about me; in His tent I will offer
sacrifices and shouting of joy; I will sing, yes, I will
sing praises to the Lord.
Hear, O Lord, when I cry aloud; have mercy and be
gracious to me and answer me!
– Psalm 27:4-7 (AMP)

David was referred to as a "man after God's own heart" for a reason. He had only one desire – to be with his Lord; to dwell in God's house and behold His beauty continually. David was like any of the rest of us. He had things to do. He had responsibilities. What he was expressing was that the Presence of the Lord was his number one priority.

Once you have witnessed the beauty of the Lord, you want to return again and again. Even if you neglect to do so, there will remain a longing in your heart to be in His Presence. There is an undeniable desire within each of us to dwell in His house. We long to behold His beauty and inquire in His temple.

There have been times of trouble and turmoil in my life. I have to admit that I didn't instantly ask God for the answers. I spent some time inquiring of friends, professionals, books, TV programs, etc. But when the Lord got my attention, and I could sense the call to come into the place where all answers are found, I said yes to the invitation. I discovered that He had just what I needed, and it was only revealed in the place of prayer. He loves to hide His children in the time of trouble, like a good parent will keep their child protected from a storm. He is our great hiding place. When you look to Him to hide you, you begin to feel safe again. You see Him as your refuge, and your rock. Your stability returns, even if your life seems like a war.

And he shall speak great words against the most
High, and shall wear out the saints of the most High
- Daniel 7:25a (KJV)

The devil uses troubled times to discourage us and wear us down. If we don't run to God, Who is our high tower, then we will become overwhelmed with discouragement. We will become weary, even in well-doing. But when we keep prayer our first priority, even during hard times, we will discover that God has lifted our heads above our enemy. The Bible says we are above only! While the enemy is below, trying to hurt and harm us, we are rising higher and higher, knowing that no weapon formed against us will prosper. The reality of this will cause us to offer sacrifices of joy. Our joy leads us to sing the high praises of God.

The high praises are the songs of expectation. What is our expectation during the time of trouble? Deliverance, of course. In the place of prayer God will show you your victory. The songs you will sing after the Lord has delivered you are the same songs you should sing by faith now, before the victory manifests.

> *When he had consulted with the people, he*
> *appointed singers to sing to the Lord and praise*
> *Him in their holy [priestly] garments as they went*
> *out before the army, saying, Give thanks*
> *to the Lord, for His mercy and loving-kindness*
> *endure forever!*
> *- II Chronicles 20:21 (AMP)*

King Jehosephat's singers were sent out solely to sing high praises to God. God used their songs to bring confusion to all who opposed the army of the Lord, and they began to devour one another. We have the same privilege when we ascend to the holy hill of God, found in the place of prayer. We need to see for ourselves what the power of the high praises of our God will do.

No Silent Seekers

One of the worst things we can do during difficulty is keep quiet. King David said, "Hear O Lord when I cry with my voice." When you lift your voice unto God, it brings a release to you, because you are releasing what is in your spirit. Victory itself is found within your spirit. Jesus said that out of our innermost being would flow a river of life.

The Word of God is full of life and power. Open your mouth and lift up your voice to release the Word of God. Only then will you behold His life and power in your situation. Bear in mind, your situation isn't as bad as the grave that Jesus was raised from, and the same spirit that raised Christ from the dead lives inside of you. When you use your voice, you'll be releasing resurrection power.

As we run this race, there will be difficult times. There will be obstacles and there will be loneliness. You will even wonder at times if it is really worth it. *It is.* Just keep running, knowing that you will win. But for now, it is time to ascend into the high place of prayer.

FIVE ESSENTIALS FOR AN EFFECTIVE PRAYER LIFE

Essential #1 - Preparation

> *Sow for yourselves according to righteousness (uprightness and right standing with God); reap according to mercy and loving-kindness. Break up your uncultivated ground, for it is time to seek the Lord, to inquire for and of Him, and to require His favor, till He comes and teaches you righteousness and rains His righteous gift of salvation upon you.*
> *– Hosea 10:12 (AMP)*

We all have areas of hardness in our lives, which can be likened to fallow ground. What is fallow ground? Is it a heart that has become as hard as stone, with no chance of God penetrating it? Is it the person who is stubborn and resists what God is saying to them? No, fallow ground is simply any area that we have allowed to be idle. It's the area we just haven't done anything with, at least for a season.

When the Bible speaks of fallow ground, it is speaking of farmland that has been idle for a period, which allows the fertility of the soil to be restored.

We've all had this experience, spiritually speaking. We know that this may be a season for spiritual growth, yet we allow that area to remain idle. Perhaps we have neglected the high place of prayer. Or maybe we have been willing to submit only certain areas of our lives to God. Whatever the case, the Lord is saying that it is time to break up the fallow ground and restore the fertility of our hearts.

When we come before the Lord, we need to ask Him to show us the areas that are not yet in full surrender to His lordship. When you pray, prepare yourself for the Holy Spirit to show you any fallow ground. Submit yourself to the voice of His Spirit so that you can prepare to sow to the spirit.

> *For he who sows to his own flesh (lower nature, sensuality) will from the flesh reap decay and ruin and destruction, but he who sows to the Spirit will from the Spirit reap eternal life.*
> *– Galatians 6:8 (AMP)*

You are sowing to the spirit, but you are also sowing to yourself. My Pastor says, "If you don't invest in yourself, no one else will." It's just like eating right and getting exercise. No matter how much someone else can encourage or provoke you, you are the only one who will make yourself do what is best for you. Runners who intend to win will sow into themselves. Prayer is your personal investment into your God-given destiny.

The preparation is like the process of plowing. It can be painful, but the rewards are wonderful. What are the rewards? The rain of God's righteousness. When we discover areas of hardness and surrender them to God, we are made aware of His righteousness again. There's nothing like knowing we're in right relationship with God in every area of our lives.

Essential #2 - Expectation

> *My soul, wait only upon God and silently submit to Him; for my hope and expectation are from Him. He only is my Rock and my Salvation; He is my Defense and my Fortress, I shall not be moved. With God rests my salvation and my glory; He is my Rock of unyielding strength and impenetrable hardness, and my refuge is in God!*
> *– Psalm 62:5-7 (AMP)*

Hebrews 11:6 says, *"He who comes to God must believe that He is, and that He is a rewarder of those who diligently seek Him."* The word "expectation" means a thing to look forward to. I do not pray because I feel an obligation to pray, but because I look forward to the rewards produced through seeking Him.

The rewards of waiting upon God are:

Stability – Life has a way of rocking my boat now and then. But when I pray, I am rewarded with the awareness that He alone is my Rock. He alone can stabilize me.

Defense – God is my guard, my shield, and my protection against the enemy. When I wait upon Him, He rewards me with the confidence that He will take care of my enemy.

Salvation – God has done for us what we could not do for ourselves. Salvation is so much more than securing a home in heaven. It is *preservation* from the enemy's plans. It is also *deliverance*. He has delivered, He is now delivering, and He will yet deliver again. God has not shut us up into the hand of the enemy. He has wrought us *healing*. You don't have to accept sickness and disease as your portion.

He is your portion. He is Jehovah Rophe – "the Lord your health." He has purchased our prosperity. Our God has plans to bless us and to prosper us, even as our soul prospers. He has provided our soundness of mind. In His Presence He rewards us with His word. His word renews our mind. The Bible says He has given us a spirit of power, a spirit of love, and a sound mind.

Glory – When His people enjoy the fullness of His salvation, then the glory of the Lord will begin to fill the whole earth. When we walk in His rewards, then the world will know that our God is God.

> *But we all, with open face beholding as in a glass*
> *the glory of the Lord, are changed into*
> *the same image from glory to glory, even as*
> *by the Spirit of the Lord.*
> *- II Corinthians 3:18 (KJV)*

When we seek Him, we can expect to experience His glory. When we behold Him, we are rewarded with change. We are changed into His image from glory to glory. Think about your last great encounter with God. You can expect to exceed that experience.

Essential #3 - Revelation

> *He reveals the deep and secret things;*
> *He knows what is in the darkness,*
> *and the light dwells with Him!*
> *– Daniel 2:22 (AMP)*

The word "revelation" means an uncovering, or an unveiling. It's a term expressive of the fact that God has made known truths and realities, which men could not discover for themselves. In the Book of Daniel, the king had

an unusual dream that left him deeply disturbed. His distur-
bance created a lot of trouble for the "wise" men,
astrologers, and soothsayers. Daniel took advantage of this
potentially grievous situation. Because he was prepared and
pure (Daniel 1:4-8), he was bold enough to procure an
appointment with the king. He then called his companions
together to pray. They praised God for His wisdom and
might, and for revealing His wisdom to them. They
proclaimed that God reveals deep and secret things. They
thanked Him in advance for making known the interpretation of the king's dream.

At the time Daniel was presented before the king, he
was only a man of captivity, but God was about to show him
off. Daniel declared to the king's wise men, astrologers,
soothsayers, and magicians, that for them it would be
impossible to reveal the secret of the dream. Then he said,
"but there is a God in heaven Who reveals secrets." Daniel
knew this God. This God remained faithful to him, even in
his captivity. God used the gift of revelation to interpret the
king's dream, and to promote Daniel and his friends. He
was given material gifts, and became a great ruler. He even
ruled over all the wise men of Babylon.

In spite of captivity, Daniel was running to win. In every
situation, he came out on top. Why? Because he was a man
of preparation, with great expectation. He ran his race with
the spirit of revelation upon his life.

Essential #4 - Inspiration

> *But there is [a vital force] a spirit [of intelligence]*
> *in man, and the breath of the Almighty*
> *gives men understanding.*
> *– Job 32:8 (AMP)*

To inspire means to inhale, to stimulate, or impel as to

some creative effort, to motivate by a divine influence, to
arouse a thought or a feeling.

> *And Moses said unto the LORD, O my Lord, I am*
> *not eloquent, neither heretofore, nor since thou hast*
> *spoken unto thy servant: but I am slow of speech,*
> *and of a slow tongue.*
> *And the LORD said unto him, Who hath made*
> *man's mouth? or who maketh the dumb, or deaf, or*
> *the seeing, or the blind? have not I the LORD?*
> *Now therefore go, and I will be with thy mouth, and*
> *teach thee what thou shalt say.*
> *- Exodus 4:10-12 (KJV)*

In the place of prayer, God will provoke us to do something great for His glory. But many times we are like Moses,
who tried to excuse himself from that which God called him
to. God spoke to this simple man and shared how He had
seen the affliction of His people. He had heard the cry of the
slaves in Egypt. He knew their sorrows and intended to
deliver them. Sounds like a great plan so far.

After God describes the kind of land that He will bring
the Israelites into, He informs Moses that He will send him
to convey this message to Pharaoh, and that he (Moses)
would bring them out. I can just imagine his response –
"Now wait a minute God! What am I supposed to say and
how am I going to say it?" Isn't that our first fear when God
calls us to do something big? How will I say to others what
God has said to me?

So Moses starts making excuses. He begins with the
obvious: "I am not eloquent." In other words, he had no
influence or effective use of language. He was afraid of
getting tongue-tied. He thought himself unfit to speak to
great men about great affairs. After all, to tell Pharaoh that
he was going to have to lose all of his slaves, just because

God said so, was a significant matter. But God cancelled all of Moses' excuses by letting him know that He would be with his mouth and teach him what to say. We know that Moses did in fact fulfill that which God called him to do. He led the Israelites out of the house of bondage. How did he do it? He accomplished the call through the inspiration of the Almighty. God breathed the words into his mouth. God showed him what to do every step of the way.

[The Servant of God says] The Lord God has given Me the tongue of a disciple and of one who is taught, that I should know how to speak a word in season to him who is weary. He wakens Me morning by morning, He wakens My ear to hear as a disciple [as one who is taught].
– Isaiah 50:4 (AMP)

You may feel like Moses, afraid of being tongue-tied. Begin confessing that God has given you the tongue of the learned. You may be surrounded by those who are weary. Wouldn't you love to see them receive an infusion of strength? God wants to use you to speak that strength into their lives. You may long to hear God the way that Moses heard Him. There may not be a burning bush, but God will awaken your ear to hear. Let Him breathe His inspiration into your spirit through an active life of prayer.

Remember, Moses had to leave the place where God gave him the marching orders. He had to step into the process of delivering God's people. He had to constantly stay open to inspiration.

When you live a life of prayer, your spirit is kept open to receiving divine inspiration, even after your initial encounter with God.

Essential #5 - Isolation

"Isolation leads to revelation." -Bishop Jack C. Wallace

For some, finding the time and the desire to be alone with God can be the most challenging call they have ever faced. You may say, "If prayer is such a great place to be, then why is it so difficult to get there?" The answer is this: you have two opponents, 1. the flesh, and 2. the devil. You must learn to deal with these two opponents in the right order.

First, deal with your own flesh. Remember when the disciples fell asleep while Jesus was praying. His response to them was, "The spirit is willing, but the flesh is weak." The willingness to be alone with God is in your spirit, not your flesh. Before you rise up to the high place of prayer, you must first let your spirit rise up to the place of prominence over your flesh.

Your second opponent is the devil. We know that he has come to steal, kill, and destroy. He wants to steal your time with God. Why? Because your potential is discovered and released in the place of prayer. Your God-given potential horrifies the devil. The spirit of the deliverer abides in each one of us. If we learn to isolate ourselves in prayer, we will be delivered ourselves. And like Moses, we will also become empowered to bring others out of bondage. That's reason enough for the devil to discourage your holy ambition to pray.

Ambition is a determination to succeed. It's the drive and zeal within us. If the devil can kill your ambition, he can destroy your destiny. Don't be ignorant of his devices, plans, schemes, or tricks. We are not to be afraid of him, but we are not to ignore the fact that he is out to destroy our destinies in God. If he can keep you from isolation (your time with God), he can keep you from your destination.

Seven keys to being alone with God

1. Get still before Him to communicate with Him. God told David to be still and know that He is God (Psalms 46:10). There is nothing more satisfying than to have God reveal Himself to you in a new measure. When you learn to enjoy your time of isolation, He will give you greater revelations of Himself. Before God reveals who we are in Him, He wants to reveal who He is in us. Revelations 3:20 tells us that Jesus stands at the door knocking. Picture yourself alone in your house. Jesus is at the door waiting for you to open it for Him. When you do, He will come in and have an intimate dinner for two with you. When you are alone, resist the temptation to become bored, or to run off and find something else to do. Seize the opportunity to cultivate your relationship with God. He is affording you the time to know Him intimately.

2. Draw near to His heart. James 4:8a says, "Draw nigh to God, and he will draw nigh to you." If you would get past the surface types of prayer when you go before the Lord, and truly begin to draw yourself toward Him, He will respond by drawing Himself toward you. Once you make known to the Lord your determination to draw near to Him, He will approach you like He did Mary. He will come proclaiming you as blessed and highly favored of the Lord. I use Mary, the mother of Jesus, to illustrate this because I know that just as the Spirit of God planted the Seed of God's own Son in her womb, He desires to plant the seed of purpose in the womb of *your* spirit.

3. Seek His Face.

> *O GOD, You are my God, earnestly will I*
> *seek You; my inner self thirsts for You, my*
> *flesh longs and is faint for You, in a dry and*
> *weary land where no water is. So I have*
> *looked upon You in the sanctuary to see Your*
> *power and Your glory.*
> *— Psalm 63:1-2 (AMP)*

When you step out to seek His face, you will find it to be friendly and welcoming. He'll invite you to express your hunger and thirst to Him. The more you seek Him, the more desperate you'll become to see His power and glory. Not only in the house of God (when the saints are all gathered to worship Him), but also in the private place of prayer.

> *Blessed (happy, fortunate, to be envied) is*
> *the man whom You choose and cause to*
> *come near, that he may dwell in Your courts!*
> *We shall be satisfied with the goodness of*
> *Your house, Your holy temple.*
> *— Psalm 65:4 (AMP)*

You are blessed of the Lord because He has chosen you and caused you to approach Him. He's invited you to dwell in His courts. When you dwell in the place where He is, you will be satisfied with the goodness of His house, even the goodness of His holy temple.

4. Spend time in His Presence.

> *And the Lord said, My Presence shall go*
> *with you, and I will give you rest. And Moses*
> *said to the Lord, If Your Presence does not*
> *go with me, do not carry us up from here!*
> *– Exodus 33:14-15 (AMP)*

Moses deliberately set up his tent a great distance from the camp, so that he could seek God. When he went into this tabernacle, God showed up in His glory to talk to him. Remember, when we draw nigh unto God, He will draw near to us. There the Lord spoke to Moses face to face, as a man speaks to his friend.

Moses put God in remembrance of His Word. He said, "If I have found grace in Your sight as you have said, then show me Your way, that I may know you." He wanted the grace to continue to lead God's people. He wanted a guarantee of God's Presence. The Lord assured him of His Presence and that he had found grace in His sight. He even knew Moses by name. After this intimate conversation, Moses must have had a new impartation of faith, for then he requested of the Lord to show him His glory.

Remember when Moses entered the tabernacle? Didn't God's glory come down? Yes, but after spending time in the Presence of the Lord, Moses wanted to move from that glory to the next realm of glory. This is what God's glory does. It compels us to ask for a deeper experience.

5. Get to know God.

> *Thus says the Lord: Let not the wise and
> skillful person glory and boast in his wisdom
> and skill; let not the mighty and powerful
> person glory and boast in his strength and
> power; let not the person who is rich [in
> physical gratification and earthly wealth]
> glory and boast in his [temporal satisfac-
> tions and earthly] riches; But let him who
> glories glory in this: that he understands
> and knows Me [personally and practically,
> directly discerning and recognizing My
> character], that I am the Lord, Who
> practices loving-kindness, judgment, and
> righteousness in the earth, for in these
> things I delight, says the Lord.
> – Jeremiah 9:23-24 (AMP)*

In this world, people will glory in many
things. If they are wise, they will glory in
their wisdom. If they are strong, they will
glory in their strength. If they are rich, they
will glory in their riches, and so on. God says
that there is but one thing to glory in, "Let
him that glories glory in this, that he knows
Me." We are invited to know the God Who
exercises loving-kindness, judgment, and
righteousness in the earth.

> *Yes, let us know (recognize, be acquainted
> with, and understand) Him; let us be zealous
> to know the Lord [to appreciate, give heed
> to, and cherish Him]. His going forth is
> prepared and certain as the dawn, and He*

*will come to us as the [heavy] rain, as the
latter rain that waters the earth.*
– Hosea 6:3 (AMP)

We need to continue on to know Him.
There should be a holy pursuit about us. For
when we seek Him, we shall find Him. When
we find Him, we can enjoy the privileges
of getting to know Him. When we become
acquainted with our God, then we will do His
will. Look at it this way: pursuing Him leads
us to intimacy, which leads to pleasing Him in
all that we do. Isn't God worthy of our searching of Him, that we may know Him? Those
who are running to win will seek the One
Who will empower them to do so.

6. Count everything as nothing in comparison to
knowing Him and beholding His glory.

*Yes, furthermore, I count everything as loss
compared to the possession of the priceless
privilege (the overwhelming preciousness,
the surpassing worth, and supreme advantage) of knowing Christ Jesus my Lord and
of progressively becoming more deeply and
intimately acquainted with Him [of perceiv-
ing and recognizing and understanding Him
more fully and clearly]. For His sake I have
lost everything and consider it all to be mere
rubbish (refuse, dregs), in order that I may
win (gain) Christ (the Anointed One)*
– Philippians 3:8 (AMP)

Whether it's your possessions, position,

power, or prestige, you should count it all as nothing in comparison to knowing Jesus. There may be times of suffering loss, but you can be sure that the temporal trouble is not worthy to be compared to the eternal glory that is before you. In Romans 8:23-24 the Holy Spirit forewarned Paul that chains and tribulation awaited him. Yet he would not be moved. He didn't even count his own life as dear. He simply wanted to finish the race with joy. Like Jesus, he wanted to do the will of his Father, which was to testify of the Gospel.

It's been said that it's not how you start, but how you finish that counts. How will you finish *your* course? Those who run well and finish their race will hear the Lord say, "Well done, good and faithful servant. Enter into the eternal glory of God."

7. Be ye filled. Remember, there is one baptism, but many fillings. You should be filled with the Holy Ghost and with His power every day. Be filled with the Word of God. King David said that he rejoiced at God's Word as one who had found great treasures. The Word is like a treasure box. It's full of the riches of God. Let God's Word dwell in you richly each and every day. Let that Word be in your mouth and in your mind so that you will *do* it. Then will you have true prosperity. Then you will run with success.

Be filled with a zeal for God, for His House, for good works, and for gifts of the spirit. If you're zealous for these things, there will be no room for the flesh or for the devil. Be filled with a compassion for the hurting and the hopeless. Let the compassion of Christ within you offer hope and healing to others. If you're full of compassion, you will speak a word in due season for those who are weary.

As a believer, what does it mean to be a winner? It means taking as many as possible with you to the finish line. It means making winners out of others by sharing the power of God's love with them. These are God's righteous ways, and if we are hungry and thirsty for righteousness, we will be filled.

I'm running to win,
Regardless of how my adversary may roar.
He is made a powerless lion,
As I declare the Word of the Lord

3 RUNNING WITH THE WORD OF THE LORD

For I [Myself] will give you a mouth and such utter-
ance and wisdom that all of your foes combined will
be unable to stand against or refute.
– Luke 21:15 (AMP)

This Book of the Law shall not depart out of your
mouth, but you shall meditate on it day and night,
that you may observe and do according to all t
hat is written in it. For then you shall make your
way prosperous, and then you shall deal
wisely and have good success.
– Joshua 1:8 (AMP)

We deal more directly with the devil in the following chapter, but we will learn to effectively deal with him by using the Word of God. The Bible says that Jesus came to give us abundant life, and the Word of God is the source of the life we long to live.

Did you know that you have the ability to change any circumstance? How? With the spoken Word of God, which is pure creative power. You can create new circumstances that will be conducive to enjoying the abundant life.

Look at the circumstances in your life. Which ones need to change? As you read on, prepare yourself to change your adverse situations. Your power to change anything is with the Word of God.

But what saith it? The word is nigh thee,
even in thy mouth, and in thy heart: that is, the word
of faith, which we preach
– Romans 10:8 (KJV)

You have the power, which is the Word, near you. How near is this power? It's in your mouth and in your heart. If you're a born-again child of God, you have a creative force within you; it is the word of faith. The apostle Paul was mightily used of God during his life. His works live on in the written Word of God. Paul said that we have the same spirit of faith as the one (King David) who said, "I believe, therefore have I spoken."

We having the same spirit of faith,
according as it is written,
I believed, and therefore have I spoken;
we also believe, and therefore speak
– II Corinthians 4:13 (KJV)

I will walk before the LORD in the land of the living.
I believed, therefore have I spoken:
I was greatly afflicted
– Psalm 116:9-10 (KJV)

What was David believing for? To see the goodness of the Lord manifest in the land of the living. He believed it, therefore he spoke it. What were his circumstances like? For him it was a time of great trouble and sorrow (Psalm 116:3). He was surrounded by a sense of death. In all of this, he still acknowledged that he had the creative power of God within him. It was the Word of faith, which is the very spirit of faith. The spirit of faith is the God-kind of expectation. He made the choice to release the word of faith with his own mouth.

Take a look at the above portion of Scripture (Psalm

116:9-10). See if you can hear King David's confession. First, when David called upon the Lord, he said, "deliver my soul." Your soul is your mind, will, and emotions. David asked for his soul to be delivered, because he knew that dwelling on the death that surrounded him would only make his outlook worse. It was wise of him to ask God to deliver his soul. Then, he declared God to be gracious, righteous, and merciful. In the midst of trouble, we must never forget God's grace and mercy. Psalm 23 tells us that grace and mercy will follow us all the days of our lives. Grace is another word for "favor." You must realize that just because you are facing difficulty, you have not fallen out of God's favor. The spirit of faith will remind you of His mercy and grace.

Later, David said that God was the One Who would preserve him. When you're faced with trouble and turmoil, or any situation that seems hopeless, set the following Scriptures before you and speak them out loud by the spirit of faith. For then the same God Who preserved David and the apostle Paul shall also keep you.

> *O love the LORD, all ye his saints:*
> *for the LORD preserveth the faithful,*
> *and plentifully rewardeth the proud doer.*
> *– Psalm 31:23 (KJV)*

God will preserve the faithful. Remain faithful to love the Lord at all times. Don't get mad at God for your troubles, love Him through them and He will keep you. The Bible tells us that He Who keeps you will not slumber or sleep. He is always mindful of your situation. He will also reward the "proud doer," which is the devil. Remember, he was lifted up in pride and cast out of heaven. He can no longer do the works he was created for (to make the sounds of pure worship). Now he is the proud doer in the earth. God shall reward him according to his deeds. A good way to resist the devil is to remind him of his future reward.

> *When the wicked, even mine enemies and my foes,*
> *came upon me to eat up my flesh, they stumbled and*
> *fell. Though an host should encamp against me,*
> *my heart shall not fear: Though war should rise*
> *against me, in this will I be confident.*
> *– Psalm 27:2-3 (KJV)*

God will never forsake you, though the enemy will at times try to make you think He will. Don't buy into that lie. God has promised never to leave or forsake His own. God's people are preserved forever. There is no need to fear. You may hear the roar of the lion (the devil). He's just making a lot of noise to try to create a spirit of fear in you. Don't accept that spirit. When you're facing adversity, or even if you're face to face with the adversary himself, you must release the spirit of faith and say: *"God will preserve me, He will not forsake me, He's not given me a spirit of fear. I have power, even the creative power of God to change any circumstance. I have love, the perfect love of God operates in my life. Perfect love casts out all fear. I have soundness of mind. I will not dwell on death, sickness, poverty, or lack of any kind. My soul has been delivered, and with soundness of mind I will meditate on His Word day and night."*

> *He keepeth the paths of judgment,*
> *and preserveth the way of his saints.*
> *– Proverbs 2:8 (KJV)*

> *For we are God's [own] handiwork (His*
> *workmanship), recreated in Christ Jesus,*
> *[born anew] that we may do those good*
> *works which God predestined (planned*
> *beforehand) for us [taking paths which He*

prepared ahead of time], that we should
walk in them [living the good life which He
prearranged and made ready for us to live].
- Ephesians 2:10 (AMP)

God has set you on the path that leads to the good life.
He does not intend to allow any trial to take you off that
path. He is faithful to preserve the way of His saints.

And the Lord shall deliver me from every evil work,
and will preserve me unto his heavenly kingdom:
to whom be glory for ever and ever. Amen.
– II Timothy 4:18 (KJV)

God still has the same ability; He has not changed. He is
able to deliver us. The devil cannot devise some new plan
that will outsmart the God of heaven, the Creator of the
universe. No weapon shall prosper against you. God shall
preserve you and deliver you out of every evil work. There
are times when we feel we've hit the lowest point in our
lives. During these times we must remember that God is our
very present help in time of need.

Thou art my hiding place;
thou shalt preserve me from trouble;
thou shalt compass me about with songs
of deliverance. Selah.
– Psalm 32:7 (KJV)

Fear thou not; for I am with thee:
be not dismayed; for I am thy God:
I will strengthen thee; yea, I will help thee;
yea, I will uphold thee with the right hand
of my righteousness.
– Isaiah 41:10 (KJV)

RETURNING UNTO YOUR REST

Return unto thy rest, O my soul;
for the LORD hath dealt bountifully with thee.
– Psalm 116:7 (KJV)

When you begin to release the spirit of faith through the spoken word of God, then you begin to enter into His rest. Trials have a way of wearing us down, making us tired. When we're resting in the Lord, He is able to reinvest His creative flow in us. In the place of rest we can receive divine inspiration. Rest can lead to revelation. Revelation is God's way of working. He reveals Himself to us as faithful and able. He reveals who we are in Him, and that nothing is impossible for those who believe. He reveals the unsurrendered areas of our lives. He also reveals the secret plans of the enemy. In the place of rest the Lord will inspire you to speak that which you are believing Him for. In that place you will be fully persuaded that the Lord has dealt bountifully with you.

How does He deal bountifully with you? By the spirit of faith, which brings you to the place of seeing greater things. Your soul no longer dwells in death. Your eyes are no longer clouded with tears. Your feet have been delivered from falling. Even when circumstances have brought you low, you can still say that God has made your feet like hinds feet, and you will climb on your high places in God.

The Lord God is my Strength, my personal bravery,
and my invincible army; He makes my feet like
hinds' feet and will make me to walk [not to stand
still in terror, but to walk] and make [spiritual]
progress upon my high places [of trouble, suffering,
or responsibility]!
– Habakkuk 3:19 (AMP)

Regardless of your circumstance, there is a high place in God for you. You're not falling. You're climbing higher and higher in Him. You've been appointed to walk before God. Trials, troubles, and adversities are not your portion in life. Your portion is in the land of the living. It is abundance and the God-kind of life. In fact, God Himself says that *He* is your portion.

> *For our light affliction,*
> *which is but for a moment,*
> *worketh for us a far more exceeding and*
> *eternal weight of glory;*
> *While we look not at the things*
> *which are seen,*
> *but at the things which are not seen:*
> *for the things which are seen are temporal;*
> *but the things which are not seen*
> *are eternal.*
> *– II Corinthians 4:17-18 (KJV)*

Although for the moment you are greatly afflicted, speak with the spirit of faith. Your temporal trouble will give place to eternal glory. Turn your eyes toward the all-wise God, Who is the Author and Finisher of your faith. By His Spirit you are empowered to release the word of faith that is near unto you. Even the word that is in your mouth and in your heart.

Remember, *this* is how to change any circumstance:

God's word is the Key
Faith is the Power
Speaking with the spirit of faith is the Way

THE WAY TO SUCCESS

Only be thou strong and very courageous,
that thou mayest observe to do according to
all the law, which Moses my servant
commanded thee: turn not from it to the
right hand or to the left, that thou mayest
prosper whithersoever thou goest.
This book of the law shall not depart out of
thy mouth; but thou shalt meditate therein
day and night, that thou mayest observe to
do according to all that is written therein:
for then thou shalt make thy way prosperous,
and then thou shalt have good success.
– Joshua 1:7-8 (KJV)

For forty years, Joshua held onto the vision of the "land of the living." Doubt, fear, and unbelief kept the people from entering into the land God called them to possess. Once Moses died, the Lord let Joshua know that it was time to cross over.

It takes faith to hold on to a precious promise of God for so many years. Joshua's great faith was proven by his ability to hold on to the promise. He had the same spirit of faith that we've seen in King David. He believed to see the goodness of the Lord in the land of the living. He was also rewarded for his faith, and he and Caleb were allowed to enter at the end of the years of wandering in the wilderness.

If you're in a wilderness experience, keep the faith. You will enter into the land which the Lord your God has called you to. Like Joshua, God is calling each of us to cross over the Jordan and possess the land of more than enough. He's calling us to receive our God-given inheritance.

What will it take to cross over? As stated before, it will take the spirit of faith. It will also take strength and courage. Obeying the word of the Lord takes supernatural strength. The arm of the flesh will fail you in your endeavors to obey God.

> *Thus saith the LORD; Cursed be the man*
> *that trusteth in man, and maketh flesh his*
> *arm, and whose heart departeth*
> *from the LORD.*
> *For he shall be like the heath in the desert,*
> *and shall not see when good cometh; but*
> *shall inhabit the parched places in the*
> *wilderness, in a salt land and not inhabited.*
> *Blessed is the man that trusteth in the*
> *LORD, and whose hope the LORD is.*
> *For he shall be as a tree planted by the*
> *waters, and that spreadeth out her roots by*
> *the river, and shall not see when heat*
> *cometh, but her leaf shall be green; and*
> *shall not be careful in the year of drought,*
> *neither shall cease from yielding fruit.*
> *- Jeremiah 17:5-8 (KJV)*

You will need to trust in the Lord and put your hope in Him. Then you will have enduring strength as Joshua did. Joshua trusted in the Lord and continued to hope in His Word. He kept his faith strong. Now, God was going to give him a fresh infusion of strength and courage through divine instruction.

The Lord directed him not to turn to the right or to the left. He must follow God's instructions precisely. Joshua knew exactly what the will of the Lord was concerning himself and all of God's people. It was to possess the land.

What would ensure his success? What will ensure *your* success as a runner for God? What will it take for you to win? Joshua 1:8 is an incredible portion of Scripture, which when followed, guarantees good success.

This book of the law shall not depart
out of thy mouth; but thou shalt meditate
therein day and night,
that thou mayest observe to do according
to all that is written therein:
for then thou shalt make thy way prosperous,
and then thou shalt have good success.
– Joshua 1:8 (KJV)

Joshua had to have a constant commitment to conform His life to the Word of God. The Word of God is quick, and full of life and power. But we have to be proactive when it comes to the promises of God. There is a process for our success, and it must be followed.

By faith we understand that the worlds
[during the successive ages] were framed
(fashioned, put in order, and equipped for
their intended purpose) by the word of God,
so that what we see was not made out of
things which are visible.
- Hebrews 11:3 (AMP)

We may read, we may even hear, but sometimes we find it difficult to speak the Word of God. Consider the power of the spoken word. God framed the world by speaking it into existence. Because we're created in His image and likeness, we also have the ability to frame the kind of world we want to live in. The words in your mouth have creative power.

The prophet Ezekiel spoke the Word as the Lord commanded him in the valley of dry bones. The valley of dry bones represented the whole house of Israel, whose hope was lost. The spoken word has the power to restore even the person who has lost all hope.

Let no corrupt communication proceed out of your mouth,
but that which is good to the use of edifying, that it may
minister grace unto the hearers.
- Ephesians 4:29 (KJV)

When the Word of God is in our mouths, instead of corrupt communications, it has the power to produce spiritual growth, and to minister grace to the hearer.

The Lord GOD hath given me the tongue
of the learned, that I should know how to
speak a word in season to him that is weary:
he wakeneth morning by morning, he
wakeneth mine ear to hear as the learned.
The Lord GOD hath opened mine ear,
and I was not rebellious,
neither turned away back
– Isaiah 50:4-5 (KJV)

It also has the power to bring supernatural strength to the one who is weak and weary. God's people should purpose in their hearts to keep the Word of God, which has the power to create, restore, build up others, and to give strength to the weary, in our mouths at all times. When we learn to practice this consistently, then we will be well on our way to having good success and winning our race.

MAKE MEDITATION ON THE WORD YOUR DAILY PRACTICE

The New Unger's Bible Dictionary gives the following definition of the word "meditation":

"A private devotional act, consisting in deliberate reflection

upon some spiritual truth or mystery, accompanied by
mental prayer and by acts of the affection and of the will,
especially formation as to future conduct."

Meditation is a duty that ought to be performed by all who aspire to succeed in their spiritual interests. Now let's consider the power of meditation.

But his delight and desire are in
the law of the Lord, and on His law (the precepts, the
instructions, the teachings of God)
he habitually meditates (ponders and studies)
by day and by night
– Psalm 1:2 (AMP)

Meditation on the Word of God has the power to make you fruitful and prosperous. If you have made the Word of God your delight, then you will think about it constantly. Many wonder why their lives are not producing fruit. The answer may be that they have never learned to practice meditation.

My mouth shall speak of wisdom;
and the meditation of my heart shall be of understanding.
– Psalm 49:3 (KJV)

If you meditate continually on the Word of God, you will keep your spirit open to understanding. The Bible tells us that in all our getting, to get understanding (Proverbs 4:7).

Brethren, be not children in understanding:
howbeit in malice be ye children,
but in understanding be men.
– I Corinthians 14:20 (KJV)

Possessing understanding is a sure sign of spiritual maturity. If we are going to win, we will have to grow up.

My soul shall be satisfied as with marrow and
fatness and my mouth shall praise thee with joyful
lips: When I remember thee upon my bed,
and meditate on thee in the night watches.
– Psalm 63:5-6 (KJV)

Meditation has the power to make you feel satisfied in God. When you're satisfied, you'll be able to offer praise unto the Lord with joyful lips.

O how I love thy law! it is my meditation all the day
– Psalm 119:97-98 (KJV)

Meditation on God's Word has the power to make you wiser than your enemy. If you want to outsmart the devil, learn to meditate on the Word of God. Remember this: there are no limitations to meditation. No one can keep you from it. No circumstance has the power to prevent you from thinking about the goodness of the Lord and the faithful promises of His Word.

Determination To Be A Doer

So many will make a mental decision to obey God, but it seems within just a day or two, they find themselves in the same old rebellious rut. They draw back from their commitment to follow the Lord, and they do not fulfill the vow they made. They've failed to keep the Word in their mouths, and to meditate on that Word.

Always remember this powerful principle:

Your tongue has the power, which is in speaking the Word of God, to guide your thoughts, emotions, and body into paths of prosperity and success. Joshua 1:8 speaks of obtaining "good success." Whenever I speak of this portion of Scripture to God's people, I ask them to raise their hand if they're not interested in becoming successful. Not one person ever has. Everyone wants to have success in life. Everyone wants the joy of winning that race.

Keep God's Word in your mouth. Exercise yourself in the spirit by releasing the word of faith. Be bold in speaking that which you are believing Him for. I'm believing to see His goodness in the land of the living.

Begin today to seize every opportunity to meditate on God's Word. Keep the goal before you and take every step toward doing what God tells you to do.

But be doers of the Word [obey the message], and not merely listeners to it, betraying yourselves [into deception by reasoning contrary to the Truth].
- James 1:22 (AMP)

We must not only hear, speak, or meditate, but also be *doers* of God's Word. It's the only way to make your way prosperous and to have good success. The only path that leads to victory is the one that is well lit with the word of God.

Thy word is a lamp unto my feet,
and a light unto my path.
– Psalm 119:105 (KJV)

He may afflict me, oppose me,
He may come with his lies.
Has he forgotten my Father's ear is open,
And He hears my every cry?

4 WINNING OVER THE ADVERSARY

And he said unto them, I beheld Satan as lightning fall from heaven. Behold, I give unto you power to tread on serpents and scorpions, and over all the power of the enemy: and nothing shall by any means hurt you.
– Luke 10:18-19 (KJV)

Many evils confront the [consistently] righteous, but the Lord delivers him out of them all.
– Psalm 34:19 (AMP)

It is reassuring to know that God hears every prayer, and when we're in times of trouble, He promises to be our very present help. The righteous will face many afflictions, and God will deliver us out of them all, but wouldn't it be nice to know how to have fewer afflictions?

The enemy comes against us in many ways, and he opposes everything we represent in God. It is important to know our identity in God, and it is equally important to know who our enemy is, so we can become effective in enforcing kingdom rule in every area he tries to manifest.

SATAN'S IDENTITY

His names reveal his very nature. When he afflicts you, you must realize that this is all he knows. His identity and purpose for existing is to come against God's people.

The Bible calls him the adversary (I Peter 5:8). Not only will he bring adversity into your life, but he will also seek to use that adversity to devour you. Jesus called the devil "the thief" (John 10:10). We know this is true. Who hasn't had the thief steal from them? He's a murderer and a liar (John 8:44). In fact, the Bible says he is the father of all lies.

He is also a deceiver (Revelations 12:9), an angel of light (II Corinthians 11:4), the prince of this world (John 12:31, John 14:30, John 16:8-11), the prince and power of the air (Ephesians 2:2), and the god of this world (II Corinthians 4:4).

THE PROVISION OF POWER

We can clearly see through the Scripture that the devil has quite the identity. The average person is intimidated by the devil, but as born again believers, we have absolutely nothing to be fearful of. The One Who watched him fall as lightening from heaven lives inside each one of us.

And the seventy returned again with joy, saying,
Lord, even the devils are subject unto us
through thy name.
– Luke 10:17 (KJV)

After Jesus commissioned the seventy, they went to various cities to heal the sick and proclaim the Kingdom of God had come. They returned with great joy, saying that even the devils were subject to them through the name of Jesus.

When they shared their experience with Jesus, it was as if He responded by saying, "Of course demons are subject to you. After all, I was right there the day Satan was kicked out of heaven." Satan knows the Son of God was in heaven the day the Father God responded to his rebellion and evicted him forever from his glorious position.

The seventy were using the Name which is above every

other name, including all sickness and demonic oppression.

SATAN – THE FALLEN FOOL

For thou hast said in thine heart, I will ascend into
heaven, I will exalt my throne above the stars of
God: I will sit also upon the mount of the
congregation, in the sides of the north:
I will ascend above the heights of the clouds;
I will be like the most High.
– Isaiah 14:13-14 (KJV)

Thou art the anointed cherub that covereth; and I
have set thee so: thou wast upon the holy mountain
of God; thou hast walked up and down in the midst
of the stones of fire. Thou wast perfect in thy ways
from the day that thou wast created, till iniquity was
found in thee. By the multitude of thy merchandise
they have filled the midst of thee with violence, and
thou hast sinned: therefore I will cast thee as
profane out of the mountain of God: and I will
destroy thee, O covering cherub, from the midst of
the stones of fire. Thine heart was lifted up because
of thy beauty thou hast corrupted thy wisdom by
reason of thy brightness: I will cast thee to the
ground, I will lay thee before kings, that they may
behold thee. Thou hast defiled thy sanctuaries by
the multitude of thine iniquities, by the iniquity of
thy traffick; therefore will I bring forth a fire from
the midst of thee, it shall devour thee, and I will
bring thee to ashes upon the earth in the sight
of all them that behold thee.
– Ezekiel 28:14-18 (KJV)

Satan was originally the anointed cherub who was set up

by God in His holy mountain. He was actually perfect until iniquity was found in him. His heart was lifted up in pride. Because he really thought he was "all that," he began to make plans according to his own will. Five times Lucifer said in his heart, "I will," and five times God responded with His own "I wills." Lucifer said, "I will ascend into heaven." God said, "I will cast you down as profane out of the mountain of God" (Ezekiel 28:16). It is interesting to note the definition of the word profane. It means not sacred, secular, irreverent, blasphemous, vulgar, and obscene. Remember, Satan is called "the god of this world." The above definition helps us to recognize his character.

Satan also said, "I will exalt my throne above the stars of God" (Isaiah 14:18), but God said, "I will destroy thee" (Ezekiel 28:16). Satan said, "I will sit upon the mount of the congregation" (Isaiah 14:13), but God said, "I will cast you down to the ground" (Ezekiel 28:17). Satan said, "I will ascend above the clouds" (Isaiah 14:14), but God said, "I will lay you before Kings." Then Satan declared his ultimate goal: "I will be like the Most High" (Isaiah 14:14), but God said, "I will bring a fire to devour him and that he would be reduced to ashes" (Ezekiel 28:18).

I call Satan "the fallen fool" because it was foolish of him to think more highly of himself than he really was. He had a prestigious position, but evidently it wasn't good enough for his prideful heart. So, Satan fell because he tried to excel in authority beyond his God-given position. He thought he had the power to rise up and be like the Most High, but no one can be equaled with God. He alone sits on His throne.

If you look at the ways Satan suffered when he fell as lightening from heaven, you can see some similarities in the way he seeks to afflict God's people. For example, he was cast out as profane. Take a look at the world around us. It's easy to see the unholy, irreverent, blasphemous, vulgar, and obscene in the society in which we live. What family hasn't been touched by the effects of sin?

Satan seeks to come against us with the very same things he suffered when he was cast out of heaven. It was declared in the heavens that Satan would be destroyed. He desperately seeks to destroy those whom God has declared to be above the angels.

Satan was cast down to the ground. The Bible tells us that we are above only, yet how many of God's people have suffered from attack in the form of depression, and even demonic oppression? God said He would reduce the devil to ashes. Isn't that what the devil tries to do to us? He attempts to devour us in the furnace of affliction, but God says He will give us beauty for ashes.

We have heard it said that when the devil reminds you of your past, you should remind him of his future. But really we should be reminding him that he has already been stripped of all his power. He lost his God-given position of authority. We, on the other hand, have been seated with Christ in heavenly places. Jesus said He gave us the power to tread over all the power of the enemy, and nothing shall by any means harm us. We are actually hidden in the One Who witnessed the fall of Satan. You need to keep the devil reminded of this. Make it your habit to resist him with your God-given authority, and he will flee from you.

RUNNING WITH A HOLY RESISTANCE

Put on God's whole armor [the armor of a heavy-armed soldier which God supplies], that you may be able successfully to stand up against [all] the strategies and the deceits of the devil.
– Ephesians 6:11 (AMP)

Those who are running to win must also know how to

resist the devil, and stand against his wiles, tricks, and schemes. We stand against and resist the devil in truth, righteousness, the gospel of peace, faith, salvation, and the sword of the Spirit.

A PEOPLE OF POWER

But ye shall receive power, after that the Holy Ghost is come upon you: and ye shall be witnesses unto me both in Jerusalem, and in all Judea, and in Samaria, and unto the uttermost part of the earth.
– Acts 1:8 (KJV)

The power of the Holy Ghost has enabled God's people to become fearless. Even if you feel like a coward, His power will give you a lion-like boldness. Remember Peter on the day of Pentecost. Acts 2:14 tells us that after being endued with power from on high, Peter (yes Peter – the one who denied the Lord three times out of fear) stood up, lifted up his voice and commanded that they hear his words. After preaching his first sermon, he gave a salvation invitation.

Then Peter said unto them, Repent, and be baptized every one of you in the name of Jesus Christ for the remission of sins, and ye shall receive the gift of the Holy Ghost.
– Acts 2:38 (KJV)

He said unto them repent, be baptized, and you shall receive the Holy Ghost. He continued to testify and exhort. He was so full of power that he couldn't stop. The people gladly received his words. Three thousand were saved just that day. Those three thousand, along with those who had received the Holy Ghost in the upper room, became the most powerful group of people the world had ever seen. All because Peter had the boldness to tell them how they could be saved, and also to receive the power of God, through the gift of the Holy Ghost.

WHEN POWER PREVAILS

When the power of the Spirit prevails in the Church, there won't be so many new converts falling away. The devil will not be as able to discourage the saints. They will get "plugged in" and become true disciples, which is the fulfillment of the great commission.

> *And they continued steadfastly in the apostles' doctrine and fellowship, and in breaking of bread, and in prayers. And fear came upon every soul: and many wonders and signs were done by the apostles. And all that believed were together, and had all things common; And sold their possessions and goods, and parted them to all men, as every man had need. And they, continuing daily with one accord in the temple, and breaking bread from house to house, did eat their meat with gladness and singleness of heart, Praising God, and having favour with all the people. And the Lord added to the church daily such as should be saved.*
> *– Acts 2:42-47 (AMP)*

Those who got saved as a result of Peter's sermon on the day of Pentecost devoted themselves entirely to the instruction and fellowship of the apostles. Not only did they learn sound doctrine, but they also were not afraid of getting to know one another. They learned how to pray together. They understood the fear of the Lord. Many signs and wonders were performed through the apostles. They shared their possessions so that everyone's needs were met. They continued in this new lifestyle daily, and were unified. They were welcomed into one another's homes and had the joy of salvation. They were people of praise and had favor with the community. In fact, more people were getting saved every day.

It is interesting to note that for the first five chapters of the book of Acts, Satan is not mentioned even once. This is because the power of God prevailed. This power produced boldness that caused a man (who was once a coward) to preach the Word with conviction. Three thousand became completely committed to God. The faith level was high. They were hearing and doing the Word. Miracles were taking place. Satan just couldn't compete with such a move.

Again, they were unified. When there is unity among God's people, the Lord commands His blessing (Psalm 131). How can Satan battle with God's commanded blessing?

And it shall come to pass, if thou shalt hearken diligently unto the voice of the LORD thy God, to observe and to do all his commandments which I command thee this day, that the LORD thy God will set thee on high above all nations of the earth: And all these blessings shall come on thee, and overtake thee, if thou shalt hearken unto the voice of the LORD thy God.
– Deuteronomy 28:1-2 (KJV)

If we would listen to God and do what He tells us to do, His blessing will come upon us and overtake us. The second chapter of Acts is a perfect picture of a blessed and victorious church. The Word says when you're blessed, your enemy will rise up against you one way, and flee from you seven ways. That's just too much devastation for the devil. So, he's going to think long and hard about rising up against a church that is blessed.

THE PATHWAY OF POWER

How do we tread and trample on the power of the enemy? By letting the power of God produce boldness and obedience in our lives. Rise up to be His witness. The devil is devastated when the church wins the lost, and when those we win allow God's power to prevail in their lives. He's devastated when we all become completely committed to the Word of God, and when we see that prayer is the privilege of every believer. Also, when we have true fellowship with one another, and care enough to share our possessions so that no one goes without. Then miracles will happen on a regular basis and souls won every day.

Those who are running to win will also have God's heart. His heart still beats for souls. Jesus wants to manifest Himself through us to win the lost and destroy the works of the devil. He sees the multitudes of unsaved people. Christ in you is still moved with compassion, and He's longing for you to offer others His abundant life. Real winners will take as many as possible with them to the finish line.

YOUR POSITION OF POWER

What's your position in Christ? Above only and in heavenly places. You are not one of Satan's victims. Whether or not you're victorious will depend on your view of yourself. You are what you think you are. Remember the men who were sent to spy out the Promised Land? They returned with an evil report of unbelief. Why? Because they saw themselves as grasshoppers, so that's how they acted. What is a grasshopper to a giant? Probably his victim. The two men of faith saw the same exact things the others saw, but their report was that they were well able to go in and possess the land. What was the difference between the doubters and the faithful? It was how they viewed themselves. Joshua and

Caleb saw the land through the eyes of promise. Regardless of what they saw in the natural realm, they had a definite "God said." They knew they were able.

You need to see *yourself* as "well able." You're not the grasshopper. You're not the victim. God has made Satan to be the grasshopper, and he's under *your* feet. You are well able to trample on all of his power. Change your view from that of a grasshopper to that of a giant; from victim to victor.

THE POWER OF LIGHT AND LIBERTY

I have chosen the way of truth:
thy judgments have I laid before me.
– Psalm 119:30 (KJV)

Now the Lord is that Spirit: and where the
Spirit of the Lord is, there is liberty.
– II Corinthians 3:17 (KJV)

When the Word of God enters your life, it brings light to every dark place. Suddenly, we are able to see the path. It brings us the hope of living the good life.

For we are God's [own] handiwork (His workman-
ship), recreated in Christ Jesus, [born anew] that
we may do those good works which God predestined
(planned beforehand) for us [taking paths which He
prepared ahead of time], that we should walk in
them [living the good life which He prearranged
and made ready for us to live].
– Ephesians 2:10 (AMP)

Ye are all the children of light, and the children of
the day: we are not of the night, nor of darkness.
– I Thessalonians 5:5 (KJV)

Because God's Word, the Gospel, has entered our lives, we are no longer children of darkness. We've been delivered out of darkness. Now we dwell in the light.

> *Then Jesus said unto them, Yet a little while is the*
> *light with you. Walk while ye have the light, lest*
> *darkness come upon you: for he that walketh in*
> *darkness knoweth not whither he goeth.*
> *– John 12:35-36 (KJV)*

If we do not walk in the light of His Word, then darkness (or the devil) will come upon us. When we fail to walk in the Word, we give Satan access. Hearing, speaking, thinking, and doing the Word of God is our greatest defense against darkness.

Jesus said that we have the light and we must believe in this light. He was speaking of Himself; He is the Living Word. To believe Him is to believe His Word, since He and His Word are one. Blessed are those who believe in the light. If you're having trouble believing, ask Him to help your unbelief. How will He help you? He will shine His Word, which is light, on your unbelief, which is darkness.

> *Again, a new commandment I write unto you, which*
> *thing is true in him and in you: because the*
> *darkness is past, and the true light now shineth. He*
> *that saith he is in the light, and hateth his brother, is*
> *in darkness even until now. He that loveth his*
> *brother abideth in the light, and there is none*
> *occasion of stumbling in him. But he that hateth his*
> *brother is in darkness, and walketh in darkness, and*
> *knoweth not whither he goeth, because that*
> *darkness hath blinded his eyes.*
> *– I John 2:8-11 (KJV)*

Remember, our greatest defense against the devil is the Word of God. We must obey God's Word if we are to be blessed with His power and His light. Disobedience and rebellion will open doors to darkness.

Except the LORD of hosts had left unto us a very small
remnant, we should have been as Sodom, and we should
have been like unto Gomorrah.
– Isaiah 1:19 (KJV)

Willingness and obedience will keep your pathway well lit. The benefit to your obedience is a life of fruitfulness.

Now unto him that is able to do exceeding abundantly
above all that we ask or think,
according to the power that worketh in us
– Ephesians 3:20 (KJV)

If you want to see God do above and beyond all that you ask or even think, then you must let His power (which is the Living Word) be at work within you.

This book of the law shall not depart out of thy
mouth; but thou shalt meditate therein day and
night, that thou mayest observe to do according to
all that is written therein: for then thou shalt make
thy way prosperous, and then thou shalt
have good success.
– Joshua 1:8 (KJV)

This is the only way to keep His power at work within you. After hearing or reading the Word, confess it, meditate upon it, and be diligent in doing it. Then you will make your way prosperous. Then you will have good success. The greatest way to overcome the adversary is to become a successful believer.

For I know the thoughts and plans that I have
for you, says the Lord, thoughts and plans for
welfare and peace and not for evil, to give you
hope in your final outcome.
– Jeremiah 29:11 (AMP)

You will never become successful until you become a partaker with the plan of God. I like to spell plan like this:

P – purpose to
L – live
A – abundantly
N – now

Abundance means more than enough. Through the Word of God, it's our privilege to have more than enough. The devil does everything to fight this reality, because he seeks out those who only have just enough. When he steals what little they do have, then they have no evidence that they're living the kind of life Jesus came to give them.

The thief cometh not, but for to steal, and to kill,
and to destroy: I am come that they might have life,
and that they might have it more abundantly.
– John 10:10 (KJV)

The devil exists to destroy you, by using whatever means necessary. But the very reason Jesus came was to give you God's quality of life. God's kind of life is abundance.

[But] he who commits sin [who practices evildoing]
is of the devil [takes his character from the evil
one], for the devil has sinned (violated the divine

*law) from the beginning. The reason the Son of God
was made manifest (visible) was to undo
(destroy, loosen, and dissolve) the works
the devil [has done].*
– I John 3:8 (AMP)

When believers live abundantly, Jesus is manifest constantly. The works of the devil will continue to be destroyed according to the living Word that is at work within us.

God is for me, not against me.
On His Word I will stand.
It's in His strength that I run,
And I am possessing the land.

5 RUNNING AND EMBRACING THE PROCESS

Many evils confront the [consistently] righteous,
but the Lord delivers him out of them all.
– Psalm 34:19 (AMP)

It is human nature to want instant rewards. We live in an instant kind of world. It's like the person who says, "Lord, give me patience, and I want it now." They don't want patience, they want an instant reward for something they have not earned.

If you've made the decision to run with God, you will win, for He has predestined it. You will be rewarded, but according to the Word of God, rewards are reserved for the diligent. You will possess the land God has called you to, but it will only be through process.

Recently, I've made some decisions to become healthy and regain strength in my body. This commitment came by way of conviction, not for the sake of vanity. Don't misunderstand me, I believe we should all look and feel our best at any age. But, this new dedication was made because I've determined to present my body to God as a living sacrifice. I was not feeling very "alive" because of constant fatigue.

I beseech you therefore, brethren, by the mercies of God,
that ye present your bodies a living sacrifice, holy, accept-
able unto God, which is your reasonable service.
– Romans 12:1 (KJV)

I also know that we are to be instruments of righteousness, and like the apostle Paul said, I want to glorify God in my body. My life is not my own; I've been bought with a price. Now that I am the temple of the Holy Ghost, I've purposed to give Him a healthy house to live in and through. The woman who is working with me told me to begin every day (before eating) with thirty minutes of aerobic exercise. Seems simple enough. Only when I began this routine, I was amazed at how winded and tired I was before the thirty minutes were up. Right away I was tempted with the thought, "What's the use?" I've never been fit or strong anyway. I should just settle for my dull old lifestyle and leave all this exercise stuff to the health nuts. I know some of them and they seem to love it. I thought, they could have my portion.

I was taking my brisk morning walk one day, and noticed a pool of stagnant water. The Lord spoke to me and said that I was not to settle for stagnation. The word stagnant means motionless, having no current (of life or action), dull and sluggish.

Keep in mind that what I'm sharing here is not to inform you of my journey of getting in shape physically. God is looking to give us a spiritual shape up. As I continued on that morning, the Lord also spoke to me about complacency and compromise. Later, I looked up the word "complacent." It means smugly self-satisfied. Then I looked up the word "smug," which means self-important and conceited. God began speaking to me about wanting to lift His people out of the mire of complacency and compromise.

This experience certainly caused me to adjust my attitude toward the call to get in shape. It also gave me a burden to pray for the Church as a whole. How many of us have settled for spiritual stagnation? How often do you sense complacency in your own life?

The Spirit of the Lord encouraged me with these following words:

It may not have happened for you before. That does not mean it can't be done. It may be a different experience, but do not be afraid of the unfamiliar, for My faithfulness will not fail you. It may be painful, but if you endure the process, I will heal you when it hurts. It may be uncomfortable. During your discomfort, I am creating a new comfort zone for you. Do not be afraid of what may be your first steps toward greatness. You must begin somewhere, why not here and now? Come and train with Me, says the Lord. While I'm training you to reign, your walk will turn into a run, for I have called you to run with Me.

With joy you shall know that I have predestined you to win. So don't hesitate to begin your journey now. The pathway you're running shall grow brighter and brighter. Glory has been set before you. Reach forth now with all that is in you, for the greater days and for greater glory.

Later that same day, the Lord continued to inspire me:

As you run, have a vision for what you really need to see and hear: the applause of heaven. While on your course, the great cloud of witnesses are cheering you on. Hear the joyful sound in your spirit and know that the light of My countenance is upon you, says the Lord.

God's words strengthened my spirit and gave me a new zeal to run (although I was just starting to walk). I could picture myself running, as well as winning the race.

THE RUNNER'S THIRST

Ho, every one that thirsteth, come ye to the

*waters, and he that hath no money; come ye,
buy, and eat; yea, come, buy wine and milk
without money and without price.*
– Isaiah 55:1 (KJV)

The first word in this verse is "Ho." No, God is not laugh-
ing here, He's trying to get the attention of the reader. This
word is designed to call attention to the importance of the
subject. It literally means "wait, stop, and listen." Before we
set off to run haphazardly, let's hear what the Lord has to say.

The subject of importance is your spiritual thirst and
hunger. We are all hungry and thirsty for something. Jesus
said that if we are hungry and thirsty for righteousness, we
will be filled.

The Scripture uses the word "thirst" to indicate intense
desire. Search your own heart. As you continue to read, ask
yourself, "How intense is my thirst for God?" To everyone
who is thirsty for the right things, God gives an invitation.

God has invited you to the waters. Here, when God uses
the word "waters," He is speaking of His abundant blessing.
I believe one of the problems in today's Christian world is
that many are ashamed to expect God's abundance.

*Bless the LORD, O my soul, and forget not all his
benefits: Who forgiveth all thine iniquities; who
healeth all thy diseases; Who redeemeth thy life
from destruction; who crowneth thee with
lovingkindness and tender mercies;
Who satisfieth thy mouth with good things; so that
thy youth is renewed like the eagle's.*
– Psalm 103:2-5 (KJV)

To be satisfied with good things is a benefit of the blessing of the Lord. According to the Word, it's when you're
mouth is satisfied that your youth is renewed. The world is

spending billions of dollars on trying to stay young. If they had the right kind of hunger and thirst, God would renew their youth.

> *They shall be abundantly satisfied with the fatness*
> *of thy house; and thou shalt make them drink of the*
> *river of thy pleasures.*
> *– Psalm 36:8 (KJV)*

What does it mean to be abundantly satisfied? It means there is divine supply out of God's abundance, and all your desires, longings, and capacities are filled. It means that God is sufficient for you. When you are abundantly satisfied, you will say (as the apostle Paul said in Philippians 4:18), I have all and abound and I am full.

The "fatness" of God's house speaks of health and vigor. Isn't that the real reason we want our youth renewed? We all want the physical strength and energy of a child.

The Word says we will drink of the river of His pleasure. The word river in Psalm 36:8 (above) is like the word waters in Isaiah 55:1. It too indicates abundance. God's pleasure for His people is that they would drink from His ever-flowing river of abundance.

> *And I will satiate the soul of the priests with fatness,*
> *and my people shall be satisfied with my goodness,*
> *saith the LORD.*
> *– Jeremiah 31:14 (KJV)*

This scripture is saying that God will satisfy the lives of His priests and His people with His abundance and goodness. God is actually out to overtake His people with blessing. He wants to fill you with good things. It's the God-kind of nourishment you'll need to win.

The Runner's Substance

It is the spirit that quickeneth;
the flesh profiteth nothing:
the words that I speak unto you, they are spirit,
and they are life.
– John 6:63 (KJV)

The runner's substance is the Word of God. His words are spirit and life. It will not profit the runner to lie on his couch and just look at his running shoes. Likewise, the flesh can profit nothing. We need the quickening Spirit of God to motivate us each day.

come ye, buy, and eat; yea, come, buy wine and milk
without money and without price.
– Isaiah 55:1b (KJV)

"Milk" in this portion of Scripture indicates a nourishing quality. When God shares His Word with us, it will strengthen and satisfy. It is substance to us.

Thy words were found, and I did eat them; and thy word
was unto me the joy and rejoicing of mine heart: for I am
called by thy name, O LORD God of hosts.
– Jeremiah 15:16 (KJV)

When you search the Scriptures for truth, you'll find the word you need, like the prophet Jeremiah. It will become the joy and rejoicing of your heart. This is the kind of joy that is not based on temporal circumstances, but on eternal evidence. His Word is the substance that has been forever settled in heaven, and through God's people, shall be established on the earth.

How sweet are thy words unto my taste!
yea, sweeter than honey to my mouth!
– Psalm 119:103 (KJV)

As newborn babes, desire the sincere milk of the word,
that ye may grow thereby
- I Peter 2:2 (KJV)

God wants you to experience the sweet substance of His Word. What milk is to a baby, the Word of God is to a believer. You will need some substance if you are going to grow up in God. As believers, we need to prioritize His Word above all else. And like Job, we must esteem the words of God's mouth even more than our necessary food (Job 3:12).

Wine symbolizes that which is cheery and invigorating to the soul. The Spirit of God is our substance of joy. On the day of Pentecost they were thought to be drunk with new wine, but they were not. They were filled with the Holy Ghost. God had satisfied them with the substance of His Spirit.

Proverbs 31:6-7 says to give wine to those who have heavy hearts, and if they drink it, they'll forget their poverty and misery.

II Samuel 16:12 also speaks of wine being given to one who has become weary in the wilderness. It seems that so many believers are suffering today with heavy hearts. Some have become impoverished and miserable. They've wandered around in a wilderness place and are weary of life.

The saints of God need to drink the wine of God's Spirit. They need to be satisfied with His substance. For heaviness, the Spirit of God will give a garment of praise. For poverty, He'll inspire you to know that He will abundantly satisfy. And for weariness, those who will drink of His wine will receive the strength of His Spirit.

Recently, I made a commitment to trade my life of mere

existence for the God-kind of life, which is abundance. I decided to exchange my weakness and weariness for the Christ kind of power, and my coldness and indifference for the Spirit's kind of fire. When a believer is running on empty, he or she needs to get filled with substance; the substance of the Holy Ghost and fire. The runner's substance is the spirit and life of God's words.

THE RUNNER'S REACH

Brethren, I count not myself to have apprehended:
but this one thing I do, forgetting those things which
are behind, and reaching forth unto those
things which are before.
– Philippians 3:13 (KJV)

I often will minister this simple illustration to those who are committed to serving God, but are still held captive to their pasts. I hold one arm behind my back with my fist tightly closed, and the other arm in front of me opened as if reaching. I let them know that they will not be able to get a hold of all that God has for them, as long as they're holding onto the past. We have to forget those things which are behind us. I like to use this phrase: "Forget it and forge on." To forge means to strive and progress. You will not have great progress in God as long as you hold on to the past, even if you're only holding on with one hand.

Wherefore do ye spend money for that which is not
bread? and your labour for that which satisfieth
not? hearken diligently unto me, and eat ye that
which is good, and let your soul
delight itself in fatness.
– Isaiah 55:2 (KJV)

What God is saying here is, "Why waste your time?" Stop spending all your strength in the past. It's like spending money for what is not bread, and laboring for that which does not satisfy.

A serious runner will listen to the words of their trainer. God wants to train us to listen to Him. When we listen and do things God's way, then we will be able to eat what is good. Our soul will delight itself in abundance. Runner's who intend to win will recognize the things that will truly satisfy. I've made reference to the one who is helping me learn how to get physically healthy and strong. I had to seek her out. I had to put forth the effort to go to her gym and get her help so that I could benefit from what she had to offer.

Seek ye the LORD while he may be found, call ye
upon him while he is near
- Isaiah 55:6 (KJV)

Prayer is not some super-spiritual, mysterious and difficult activity. God is not playing hide and seek. No, *"He is near and all who seek Him, find Him. And when they find Him, He shows them great and mighty things"* (Jeremiah 29:12).

Seeking God is never in vain. Don't buy the lie that God will not listen and answer your prayer. When we come to God, we must be committed to doing things His way. First, you must die to your flesh, because flesh can never find it's way into the presence of the Lord. Second, we must not be looking for an experience. We must seek Him in faith. The walk of faith will sometimes be void of feelings. We must be faithful, with or without the feelings. Understanding this will help us to discipline ourselves in such a way that we'll always be devoted to seeking God, regardless of how we feel. Remember, runners don't always feel like training.

I'm not belittling "experiences," we should have many

encounters with God. We just have to be sure not to rely on the experience, but on God Himself. Every experience should be confirmed with His Word. Whatever is from God has a purpose, and it should be supported with a promise. The promise must always hold a higher priority.

> *Quicken me after thy lovingkindness; so shall I keep*
> *the testimony of thy mouth. For ever, O LORD, thy*
> *word is settled in heaven.*
> *– Psalm 119:88-89 (KJV)*

We must rely upon the Word of God. We cannot just read the Word or hear it. We must walk in obedience to it. Obedience to the words that come from His mouth will preserve and keep you. We also must forsake all for Him. We must forsake our own ways, opinions, and ideas, and follow Him and His way.

> *Let the wicked forsake his way, and the unrighteous*
> *man his thoughts: and let him return unto the*
> *LORD, and he will have mercy upon him; and to*
> *our God, for he will abundantly pardon*
> *– Isaiah 55:7 (KJV)*

Our ways and thoughts are not like His, so we must forsake them. King David said that he hated every false way. Your own natural ways are not the ways of truth. In the above scripture the word "wicked" represents the more open sins. The word "thought" is the more subtle working of sin. We must turn daily to the Lord, knowing that His mercies are new every morning. He will always freely forgive when we forsake our own ways. When seeking God, always be sure to ask the Holy Spirit to search you and show you if there is any wicked way in you. Don't be discouraged if He shows you some sin. Just repent, turn, and forsake any revealed sin, so that you can enter into the presence of the Lord without shame.

THE RUNNER'S RAIN

For as the rain cometh down, and the snow from heaven, and returneth not thither, but watereth the earth, and maketh it bring forth and bud, that it may give seed to the sower, and bread to the eater
– Isaiah 55:10 (KJV)

When God rains his Word upon us, it is to accomplish something that will glorify God. Jesus said, *"Ye have not chosen me, but I have chosen you, and ordained you, that ye should go and bring forth fruit, and that your fruit should remain: that whatsoever ye shall ask of the Father in my name, he may give it you"*(John 15:16). His Word produces fruit in our lives. It is the source of spiritual rain that causes the barren to become fruitful.

THE RUNNER'S GUIDE

But the anointing which ye have received of him abideth in you, and ye need not that any man teach you: but as the same anointing teacheth you of all things, and is truth, and is no lie, and even as it hath taught you, ye shall abide in him.
– I John 2:27 (KJV)

Your guide is the anointing, which is the presence of the Holy Ghost in you. Your guide abides in you. The anointing of God will enable you to receive His teaching, like the dry and thirsty land receives the rain of heaven.

My doctrine shall drop as the rain, my speech shall

distil as the dew, as the small rain upon the tender
herb, and as the showers upon the grass.
- Deuteronomy 32:2 (KJV)

By way of revelation, God is raining upon the Church today. If we are not anointed with the power of the Spirit, we will miss it altogether. The abiding anointing is our teacher. What is it that makes a good teacher? It's the ability to teach in such a way that even a child can understand. In God, our ability to receive is not based on how old we are. God shows no partiality. The above verse speaks of abundant rain on tender plants. You may be like a child, and in some ways like a tender plant, but when God pours out His abundant rain, you will begin to flourish.

The righteous shall flourish like the palm tree:
he shall grow like a cedar in Lebanon.
Those that be planted in the house of the LORD
shall flourish in the courts of our God.
- Psalm 92:12-13 (KJV)

The runner who has demonstrated his hunger, and has been satisfied with the substance of the Spirit and the Word, is always reaching for more of God. He will receive the rain of God's abundance, have the anointing of God, and receive his reward. He is rewarded with the joy of being useful to God and flourishing. To flourish means to grow vigorously, to thrive, to prosper, and to be successful. They shall continue as a strong source of influence, even in their old age.

They shall still bring forth fruit in old age; they
shall be fat and flourishing.
- Psalm 92:14 (KJV)

They shall be fat, flourishing, and fruitful. They shall be

as strong as a cedar in Lebanon. If God's people will wait on Him, then their strength will be renewed. You must know that many will choose to flounder, meaning they will struggle in the mud – the mire of complacency and compromise. Winners, however, must flourish and be fruitful until they finish their race.

Here again, we come to the term "fat." Of course runners cannot afford to be physically fat, but those who intend to win cannot afford to live any other way, but to be abundantly satisfied with the fatness of God's house.

I've been promised an inheritance,
I'm a joint-heir with Him.
I've been guaranteed victory,
I can do nothing but win!

6 WINNING WITH THE RIGHT SPIRIT

In order to win this race, we will need to develop the spirit of a true conqueror. I can think of no greater example than that of Joseph. There are three things that come to mind when I think about this man. His dream never died, his destiny would not be denied, and he always did more than just survive. Here's a quick summary of his life...

He goes from receiving a prophetic dream and being Daddy's favorite boy to being hated by his brothers, and thrown in a pit. He is then sold into slavery, where he is eventually put in charge. He is later falsely accused and sent to prison, where he is put in charge again. He goes from the prison to the palace overnight, and in the end saves his entire family during a famine. His life is a perfect picture of the strength that resides in a person with the spirit of a true conqueror. There was something on the inside of Joseph that left him with no options. He could do nothing but win.

Take a second look at his life. It really seems to consist of two things: falling and favor. When Joseph fell, he fell hard. Not because of sin, but because there was so much opposition against him. But when he got back up, he did it with undeniable evidence that God's favor was upon his life. Consider this, he has his father's favor, but then he falls prey to his brothers' hatred and they throw him into a pit. Favor gets him out, but then he falls right into slavery. Because he is wise and discerning, favor gets him a position of authority. Then he falls into prison because of a false accusation. But because he maintained his integrity, he is once again exalted in the eyes of the governor and other prisoners. They even entrusted him with *their* dreams.

Though he continued to maintain his godly character, he was forgotten and left in the prison for two years. Then, at the appointed time, the favor of God exalted him to the highest possible position in the land. We can clearly see that this man started out low, but ended up living large and in charge.

By this I know that thou favourest me, because mine
enemy doth not triumph over me.
And as for me, thou upholdest me in mine integrity,
and settest me before thy face for ever.
- Psalm 41:11-12 (KJV)

This should encourage us all. No matter how hard you fall, even if it's no fault of your own, the favor of God will lift you up. Your enemies will not triumph over you. God's ultimate goal is for us to live our lives large, and to be in charge. God wants us to finish our course in favor. So let's learn from Joseph how to travel this sometimes difficult pathway to the palace.

NEVER ACCEPT DEFEAT

Looking unto Jesus the author and finisher of our
faith; who for the joy that was set before him
endured the cross, despising the shame, and is set
down at the right hand of the throne of God.
- Hebrews 12:2 (KJV)

Jesus is the Author and Finisher of our faith. Though we may fail at times, He hasn't written defeat into our lives. We can learn from Joseph's awesome attitude. He never counted himself as a failure. He simply would not accept defeat, even when he was rejected by his own brothers. Many born again believers have allowed rejection to rule their lives. In reality, we're all going to experience it. As Christians, we want to be Christ-like. But remember, nobody was rejected like Jesus was, and the servant is not better than his master. Let's consider how natural it was for Joseph's brothers to reject him. They were his half-brothers, and Joseph was the son of Rachel, who was the love of Jacob's life. He had his father's favor. I say this because it helps us to remember that the natural man cannot receive the things that are spiritual. So we should go ahead and face the facts now. Not everyone is going to support our dreams and visions. It is very natural for an unsaved person or carnal Christian to reject us. True conquerors will accept it, and pursue their God-given dream in spite of those who reject them.

For our light affliction, which is but for a moment,
worketh for us a far more exceeding
and eternal weight of glory;
While we look not at the things which are seen, but
at the things which are not seen: for the things
which are seen are temporal; but the things which
are not seen are eternal.
- II Corinthians 4:17,18 (KJV)

You may be in a pit right now, but you're not alone. The One Who promised to stay closer than a brother is with you. He is your Friend Who will cause you to see your affliction as momentary. Compared to the grand scheme of the rest of your life, it is but a light thing. Believe it or not, it is working for you an eternal weight of glory. The pit is not God's ultimate plan for your life. It's temporary. Everyone who has ever walked in their God-given purpose has had to find their way out of a pit or two. So take your eyes off the pit and fix them on the promise. The promise of God is what ultimately got Joseph out of the pit. He could not despair.

He only counted God, the One Who gave the promise, as faithful.

> *Faithful is he that calleth you, who also will do it.*
> *- I Thessalonians 5:24 (KJV)*

It is your attitude, while you're in the low places, that will prepare you to walk in the manifested promises later on. He will do what He promised, but for now we need to keep our attitude in proper alignment.

Did you know that the devil is the accuser of the brethren? And sisters, you have not been left out. It's his job to see to it that you are falsely accused at one time or another. You may never be forced into a room with cinderblock walls and iron bars, but the devil will be faithful in his efforts to put you in some dark prison of despair. Because we're created to be free, there's nothing worse than confinement. If that's the place you're in, reflect on what the apostle Paul said while he was in prison:

> *For that [Gospel] I am suffering affliction and even*
> *wearing chains like a criminal. But the Word of God*
> *is not chained or imprisoned!*
> *- II Timothy 2:9 (AMP)*

What do you feel is confining you right now? Is it money? A family member? Is it time, age, gender, location, or position in life? Say to that prison: "The Word of the Lord is not chained or imprisoned." Whether it's rejection, a pit, or a prison, never accept defeat. There is a living word in you, and though it may be tried, God will see to it that it is fulfilled.

Always Stand Up and Stand Out

*Even so ye, forasmuch as ye are zealous of spiritual
gifts, seek that ye may excel to the
edifying of the church.*
- I Corinthians 14:12 (KJV)

You may say, how do I stand up and stand out? Begin
right here and now to believe that God will use you. The
reason why God wants us to be zealous for spiritual gifts is
because they are His greatest source of power in bringing
truth to others. Truth is what sets people free. The gifts of
the Holy Spirit were in operation in the Old Testament as
well as the New Testament church. The gifts are about
saving lives. As mentioned earlier, we've been blessed with
all spiritual blessings. These blessings will empower us to
make a mark for our Master, as we stand up and stand out
right where we are.

Joseph's name was changed to Zaphnath-paaneah when
he went to Egypt. That name means "sustainer of life."
Remember, the gifts are about saving lives. Through
Joseph's use of spiritual gifts, not only was life in Egypt
preserved, but also Joseph's family, and even other coun-
tries, came to him to buy food during the famine.

Never Underestimate Discernment

*Discretion shall preserve thee,
understanding shall keep thee:
To deliver thee from the way of the evil man,
from the man that speaketh froward things
- Proverbs 2:11-12 (KJV)*

The root of the word discretion is "discreet," which
means to show oneself discerning, attentive, and to consider

diligently. It also means to teach or instruct. If you are wise and discerning, then God will elevate you to an influential position.

God also wants you to be attentive. Pay attention to the many possible ways God will use you to touch lives. Purpose within yourself to stop missing divine appointments. I'm certain that as a slave, Joseph was paying attention. He was probably always looking for ways to make things run more efficiently. When he was in prison, he took time to listen to the concerns of others. His discerning and attentive spirit kept him from slipping into depression over his own situation. Recently, I shared with a woman in my office, who was crying over her circumstances, that it is not hard to find someone who is in a worse situation than we are. If we would find a way to minister to that person, we could overcome our own obstacles. We will see God make a way of escape for us. My Pastor often says that what you make happen for others, God will make happen for you. If you ask in faith, God will give you a revelation for other people's problems. And all the while God will work in your life to prepare you for promotion, as you minister to others. During times of difficulty, say this: "If I want elevation, then I must get my eyes off my situation, rest under the spirit of revelation, so I can get the promotion that will take me to my destination."

> *My son, attend unto my wisdom,*
> *and bow thine ear to my understanding:*
> *That thou mayest regard discretion,*
> *and that thy lips may keep knowledge.*
> *- Proverbs 5:1-2 (KJV)*

In all the places we find Joseph along his pathway to the palace, we never once hear of him talking about his past difficulties. He guarded the knowledge he had about his own abuses. Contrary to the opinions of many, you don't always have to talk about your past pain. Your past has no power over you. You will conquer the past when you begin to live in present day power. Let your lips guard the knowledge you have of your past. Let them speak of the glorious power that God is using to work in your life today.

Have you ever heard the expression, "There's a reason why we have two ears and one mouth?" It's so we can listen more, and speak less. If you want to have the spirit of a true conqueror, you'll need to listen and pay attention to wisdom and understanding. If you're still emotionally wounded from the past, then by all means, find a safe place (perhaps with a minister or Christian counselor). Find a place to process your experience, and at the same time ask God to set a guard about your lips. We must not give the devil an opportunity to make us think our past has the power to repeat itself. There is no prosperity in the past!

The Bible tells us that Joseph always prospered. But how can a person prosper in a pit or a prison? It's all in the attitude. Your actions will follow your outlook. Joseph prospered because of his constructive point of view. He never acted like an overworked slave, or like a confined prisoner. He acted like a man who was appointed to rule.

And Joseph called the name of the firstborn Manasseh:
For God, said he, hath made me forget all my toil,
and all my father's house.
And the name of the second called he Ephraim:
For God hath caused me to be fruitful
in the land of my affliction.
- Genesis 41:51-52 (KJV)

Joseph's first son was named Manasseh, which means, "forget all my troubles and my father's household." His second son was named Ephraim, meaning "God has made me fruitful in the land of suffering." The apostle Paul said, *"This one thing I do forgetting that which is behind..."* As true conquerors we will have to forget the past, especially the pain that came from our families or significant others. The Bible clearly tells us that God has chosen us to be fruitful (John 15:16), and that we should still be fruitful in our old age (Psalm 92:14).

Many believers are under the impression that before you can be fruitful, you will have to be healed of all the emotional wounds of the past. A lot of us have gone through great difficulties, yet we would not dare to compare our lives with Joseph's. I'm not trying to discount anyone's pain, but most of us have not been put in a pit, made a slave, or spent time in a prison.

There seems to be an entire movement these days addressing issues like how to overcome your past, healing for the emotionally wounded, breaking generational curses, etc. Of course there is a place for all of the above, however I would like to use the Word of God to provoke you to know what God's priority for your life is. It is not that God doesn't want you healed. Isaiah 53:3-5 tells us that He (Jesus) was acquainted with our grief and that He cared for our sorrows. The chastisement of our peace was upon Him and by His stripes we are healed. The stripes He took were for our emotional well being, as well as our physical healing. Today, I believe that God wants to pronounce a blessing over your life; a blessing of fruitfulness and healing. You may be surprised as you see God's order of priority in the blessing.

And Joseph said unto his father, They are my sons,
whom God hath given me in this place. And he said,
Bring them, I pray thee, unto me,
and I will bless them.
- Genesis 48:9 (KJV)

*And when Joseph saw that his father laid his right
hand upon the head of Ephraim, it displeased him:
and he held up his father's hand, to remove it from
Ephraim's head unto Manasseh's head.
And Joseph said unto his father,
Not so, my father: for this is the firstborn;
put thy right hand upon his head.
And his father refused, and said, I know it, my son,
I know it: he also shall become a people, and he
also shall be great: but truly his younger brother
shall be greater than he, and his seed shall
become a multitude of nations.
And he blessed them that day, saying, In thee shall
Israel bless, saying, God make thee as Ephraim and
as Manasseh: and he set Ephraim before Manasseh.
- Genesis 48:17-20 (KJV)*

Manasseh was Joseph's first born. Remember that his
name meant, "God has made me forget all my troubles..." It
was assumed that the first-born would have the right hand
(the more significant hand) of blessing laid upon him.
Assumption can still be a dangerous thing. It is a common
assumption among believers that you cannot become fruitful
for God until you have first been healed of your past. Again,
Ephraim's name meant, "God has made me fruitful in the
land of my suffering." When Jacob blessed Joseph's sons in
this order instead of the birth order, it was a prophetic act,
and a profound lesson for us. The Scripture says that he put
Ephraim in front of Manasseh. I wonder how many believers
would be healed, if they took this illustration to heart. So
many today are too preoccupied with their pasts that they're
losing precious opportunities to glorify God with any real
productivity. Nothing will heal the pain of your past like
producing fruit in the present. Just as Manasseh and Ephraim
were the fruit of Joseph's faithfulness, so shall fruitfulness

and healing be rewards for *your* faithfulness.

God is looking for you to be faithful right where you are. If you will faithfully hold fast to that which He's given you, you will also prosper in all that you do. If you're beginning to realize that God intends for you to win, then begin today to rule where you are. Like Joseph, God has ordained for you to rule in the earth.

If you're in a pit, then rule your own heart. Don't meditate on your mess. Meditate on the original message that came from God, and don't accept defeat. Don't let that pit have any power over your God-given dream.

If you're feeling like a slave to your current circumstances, then rule as a good steward of the gifts of God. There's an anointing in you that can make things better. If you're in a prison, a place of confinement, ask God to use you anyway. Dare to believe that God could give you a word of wisdom or a word of knowledge to comfort someone else. You can rule in the spiritual realm, as well as the natural realm. Remember, the Word of God is not imprisoned. If you would become determined to be the express image of freedom wherever you are, you will, through process, be promoted to the palace. In the palace lies is the potential to rule over nations.

Regardless of setbacks,
The Lord again will appear,
To encourage and strengthen,
And say that He is near.

7 RUNNING TOWARD THE LAND OF ABUNDANCE

Can you imagine what it was like to go into the promised land as a spy, and then have to wait forty more years to go into that land to live? Caleb knew the Israelites were well able to possess Canaan as their own, but because of the opinion of the majority, his God-given promise was delayed. The Bible says that hope deferred makes the heart sick. On what must have been one of the most disappointing days of his life, how did Caleb keep himself from losing all hope? I believe part of the answer is that Caleb took what God said very seriously. His life illustrates seven principles for possessing your God-given promises.

The first principle is a challenge. I want to provoke you to recapture what God has spoken to your heart concerning your destiny. What are the original desires of your heart? In all the business of life, in all the changes, we must not lose our sense of personal identity. Seek God and ask Him to give you the grace to recapture your destiny. What has God said, and what are you doing about it?

Many years ago, when I was a very young believer, I remember a particular day I was at a carnival with a group of friends. I shared the plan of salvation with a group of young people. As I was speaking to them, God began speaking to me about my future. At that moment, God let me know that I would live my life serving Him on a full-time basis. From that day on, I knew that nothing else would fulfill me; I would obey the Lord and His call.

It would be many years before I would actually step into

a full-time ministry position, but I can honestly say that I became proactive in what God had said. Basically, whatever I could find to do, I did it wholeheartedly as unto the Lord. Through a zeal for God and a willingness to do whatever He put before me, I was able to obtain many different ministry experiences, all of which had a special part in the fulfillment of my destiny. I was simply determined to remember what God said, and do something about it.

But be ye doers of the word, and not hearers only,
deceiving your own selves.
- James 1:22 (KJV)

It's important not to be a hearer only, but also a doer of the Word. When you keep what God has said ever before you, you will find yourself doing something every day toward your God-given desire. Even if you just pray about it or meditate on it, you will, to some degree, be proactive in pursuing the promise. I believe at the end of each day we should sense the Lord saying, "Well done good and faithful servant."

At the end of the apostle Paul's life, he was able to say that he had fought the good fight and finished the course. What a great assessment for a man to have of himself. The grace to fight such a good fight came from his ability to hold on to his "God-said."

But rise, and stand upon thy feet: for I have
appeared unto thee for this purpose, to make thee a
minister and a witness both of these things which
thou hast seen, and of those things in the which I
will appear unto thee
- Acts 26:16 (KJV)

Jesus said, "I have appeared unto you for a purpose." You may not have been knocked off a horse, or heard the audible voice of God, but spiritually speaking God *has* "appeared" to you. He has made Himself known to you, and it was for a very specific purpose.

> *For if I [merely] preach the Gospel, that gives me*
> *no reason to boast, for I feel compelled of necessity*
> *to do it. Woe is me if I do not preach the*
> *glad tidings (the Gospel)!*
> *- I Corinthians 9:16 (AMP)*

Has God's mandate become a necessity to you, like preaching was to Paul? Have you come to realize that you will never be satisfied doing anything else, other than what God has put in your heart?

The word "compel" means, "to drive" or "urge forcefully or irresistibly." The apostle Paul had a holy urgency about him. He didn't resist God, and he didn't have to brag about obeying. It was as necessary to his spirit as breathing was to his body. Just as he was a messenger of glad tidings, all of our lives should be expressions of the good news, which is the gospel of the kingdom.

NEVER SETTLE FOR LESS THAN GOD'S BEST

It was said of Caleb that he was a man of a different spirit. He was not the kind of person to settle for less. I believe his tenacity positioned him to receive a grace that would cause forty years to seem like twenty. We should never underestimate the power of God's grace. It will empower you to seek, without shame, the very best God has to offer. For example, the Bible says the best spiritual gift is the gift of prophecy. Prophecy is wonderful because it builds, encourages, and comforts God's people. It is truly a blessing, one that brings supernatural strength to the Body of Christ. Yet, there are so many people who would not dare to ask God for this spiritual gift.

> *But earnestly desire and zealously cultivate the*
> *greatest and best gifts and graces (the higher gifts*
> *and the choicest graces). And yet I will show you a*
> *still more excellent way [one that is better by far*
> *and the highest of them all—love].*
> *- I Corinthians 12:31 (AMP)*

There are many believers who will disapprove of those who will actually ask God to give them any of the spiritual gifts, especially the "best" gift. They would view them as prideful or arrogant. Usually these same people will see themselves as too humble to ask for such a thing. First of all, let me give you my definition of false humility. It is refusing to accept anything that God says can be yours, and calling it humility. Thank God our confidence is in the Word of God, not the opinions of others. Those who are not walking in the spirit will often mistake confidence for arrogance. But confidence is simply accepting what God says can be yours, then seeking to excel in that very thing.

> *For to be carnally minded is death;*
> *but to be spiritually minded is life and peace.*
> *- Romans 8:6 (KJV)*

The Bible clearly tells us that to be carnally minded is death. Those who are not living the kind of life God intended are not usually happy about others who do. Conversely, to be spiritually minded is life and peace. We need to accept a Biblical fact here. Your destiny is not dependant upon your natural ability, but on your spirituality.

> *Blessed be the God and Father of our*
> *Lord Jesus Christ,*

who hath blessed us with all spiritual blessings
in heavenly places in Christ
- Ephesians 1:3 (KJV)

There's a reason why God would say we've been blessed with all spiritual blessings. Not every born again believer comes to God with built-in natural ability. Some of us have no developed skills, no known talent, and most of us are clueless as to what we were born for. But through God, we've all been blessed with spiritual blessings in Christ Jesus. My Pastor has said that God does not call the qualified, but He qualifies the called.

The God-kind of life is a life of abundance. Operating in spiritual blessing is the key to abundance. It is not arrogant to believe God for abundance, unless you're looking to heap it upon yourself. The Bible says that we are blessed to be a blessing. Spiritual blessing is all about blessing others. The best spiritual gifts are used to build up, encourage, and comfort the Body of Christ. For this reason God wants this principle solidified in your spirit: Never settle for less than God's best.

PRESS TOWARD THE MARK

Brethren, I count not myself to have appre-
hended: but this one thing I do, forgetting
those things which are behind, and reaching
forth unto those things which are before,
I press toward the mark for the prize
of the high calling of God in Christ Jesus.
Let us therefore, as many as be perfect, be
thus minded: and if in any thing ye be other-
wise minded, God shall reveal even this unto
you. Nevertheless, whereto we have already
attained, let us walk by the same rule, let us

mind the same thing.
- Philippians 3:13-16 (KJV)

Like the apostle Paul, none of us have actually apprehended all that God has for us. There is still more to reach
for. One of the things that will deplete us of needed strength
to go forward is looking back into the past. We must realize
that the only way to keep the past powerless is to let it go.
Take a good look at this scripture: *"...and reaching forth for*
the things which are before us..." Do you realize the things
that God has purposed for your life are before you right
now? You don't have to invent them or create them. They
are already there. It has been left up to us to reach for them.

Remember the movie "Rocky?" What I remember most
was the training, the suffering, and the horrible pain that he
had to endure before he even entered the ring. What was he
doing? He was pressing. That's what *our* "reaching forth" is
like. We are pressing for the mark of the prize of the high
calling. What is the mark we are pressing toward? For me it
is this: the Manifested Anointing of the Revealed Kingdom.

For the earnest expectation of the creature waiteth
for the manifestation of the sons of God.
- Romans 8:19 (KJV)

And heal the sick that are therein and say unto them, the
kingdom of God has come nigh unto you.
- Luke 10:9 (KJV)

Did you know that the earth is waiting for you to manifest as the son of God? The sons of God will demonstrate
the anointing and authority of the kingdom. When Jesus
sent the seventy in Luke 10, He gave them all power and
authority to heal the sick and cast out demons. He instructed
them to say, "The kingdom of God has come nigh unto

you." Why would He have them say this? Because in the kingdom of heaven there is no sickness, and there are certainly no demons. Declaring the presence of the kingdom is a matter of authority. Anointed people carry kingdom reality. When they encounter something that is contrary to the kingdom, they can reach beyond all human reason into the realm of divine provision.

And the LORD answered me, and said,
Write the vision, and make it plain upon tables,
that he may run that readeth it.
For the vision is yet for an appointed time, but at the
end it shall speak, and not lie: though it tarry, wait
for it; because it will surely come, it will not tarry.
- Habakkuk 2:2-3 (KJV)

Let's return to this thought for a moment. What has God said and what are you doing about it? We may not all have actual visions, but I do believe God has spoken destiny into all of our lives. His spoken words begin to reveal a vision for your life. It would serve you well to write that vision down. Make it plain enough so when you read it, you will feel empowered to run. If you keep running day after day toward your God-given vision, one day it will begin speaking. By this I mean it will be spoken through the mouths of others, who have witnessed the kind of life you live. They will begin to say the exact things you have held in your heart for years. The Lord encouraged me one day and said that when others begin speaking what you have been seeing, then you can expect for that vision to come to pass. So don't look back. Keep pressing for the manifested anointing of the revealed kingdom. Rewrite that vision, and recapture your dream today. May you receive a fresh infusion of faith to move forward in His Name.

MAKE SURE THERE'S NO SHAME IN YOUR GAME

Study and be eager and do your utmost to present yourself to God approved (tested by trial), a workman who has no cause to be ashamed, correctly analyzing and accurately dividing [rightly handling and skillfully teaching] the Word of Truth.
- II Timothy 2:15 (AMP)

My simple definition of "rightly dividing the Word of Truth," is knowing how and when to use the Word of God. We must never use the Word to neglect our God-given responsibilities. The Word of God was sent to liberate us, but we are never to use our liberty as an occasion for the flesh.

A false balance and unrighteous dealings are extremely offensive and shamefully sinful to the Lord, but a just weight is His delight.
- Proverbs 11:1 (AMP)

Those who desire to be the Lord's delight must be determined to live a balanced life. Even our spiritual lives can be a balancing act sometimes. For example, I would love to spend my entire day off just relaxing and reading my Bible, enjoying worship, and meditating on the Word. While all of this is wonderful, I cannot afford to neglect my other responsibilities. I must keep my life in balance. Those whose lives are balanced will never be referred to as "too heavenly minded to be any earthly good." If you are skilled in knowing when and how to use the Word of God, you will have nothing to be ashamed of.

TAMING YOUR FLESH

Know ye not that they which run in a race run all,
but one receiveth the prize?
So run, that ye may obtain.
And every man that striveth for the mastery is
temperate in all things. Now they do it
to obtain a corruptible crown;
but we an incorruptible.
I therefore so run, not as uncertainly; so fight I,
not as one that beateth the air:
But I keep under my body, and bring it into
subjection: lest that by any means, when I
have preached to others,
I myself should be a castaway.
- I Corinthians 9:24-27 (KJV)

This scripture tells us to run in such a way as to obtain the prize. If you have lost your ability to be temperate, or have self-control, you're really saying that you've given place to the spirit of defeat. You've begun to believe that you're not going to win anyway. So why bother showing any self-control? Now, we are not in competition (especially with one another), but we are running a race. So, we must not neglect this fruit of the spirit.

The Nelson New Illustrated Bible Dictionary says that through temperance the Christian disciplines the body and the spirit so that he is more capable of striving for his spiritual reward. I Corinthians 9:27 (above) tells us why Paul would put his own body through so much. He did not want those who had received the truth of his message to watch him become a spiritual castaway. God has called all of us to some level of leadership. You may not realize it, but you are setting an example for someone. Let's run in such a way that others will know what it will take to win this race called the Christian life.

The Bible tells us to count the cost. One thing I can promise is that it will cost you self-denial and discipline, but remember this: the goal of every new discipline is freedom!

STOP DOGGING YOURSELF FOR BEING DIFFERENT

But my servant Caleb, because he had another
spirit with him, and hath followed me fully, him will
I bring into the land whereinto he went;
and his seed shall possess it.
(Now the Amalekites and the Canaanites
dwelt in the valley.)
To morrow turn you, and get you into the wilderness
by the way of the Red sea.
- Numbers 14:24-25 (KJV)

Out of twelve men that were sent to Canaan to spy out the land, only two came back with a good report. Caleb, along with Joshua, knew that it was time to go in and possess his God-given inheritance. All the rest returned with an evil report that made the hearts of the people melt with fear. What made Joshua and Caleb so different? After all, they all went to the same land and saw the same thing.

I've heard it said of Joshua that he was equaled to every emergency. But what about Caleb; what was so great about this man? After preparing a message about this portion of Scripture, I thought that (just for fun) I'd look up the meaning of the names of each of the twelve spies. It always seems that Israelites had significant meanings for their names. It was an interesting discovery:

Shaphat – God Judges
Igal – God Redeems
Oshea – Deliverer
Palti – Delivered

Gaddiel – God Is My Fortune
Gaddi – Fortunate
Ammiel – People Of God
Sethur – Hidden
Nahbi – Concealed or Hidden
Giuel – Hidden
Joshua – The Lord Is My Salvation

Each name had an incredible meaning. According to Scripture, the Israelites felt that a good name was rather to be chosen than great riches. What was so interesting about this little name search was that Caleb's name meant "Dog, or As Canine Madness." I thought, well that's different, but what's God trying to show me? First of all, the Lord reminded me of police dogs.

My friend's father is a retired narcotics officer. He explained that once the dog has a scent of the narcotic, that scent never leaves their system until they've finally found it.

I was also reminded of a dog my family used to own when I was very young. Rusty was a small Pekinese that may have weighed all of eight pounds, but he surely must have thought he was a German Shepherd. Rusty would jump all the big dogs in the neighborhood, as if he would win every fight. Of course, he never won. He would come home whimpering and licking his wounds. But that never stopped him. He would go right back out there every chance he got to try to fight those big dogs. We would wonder, "What is wrong with this dog?" He just had a different spirit. While thinking about the meaning of Caleb's name, the Holy Spirit reminded me of this scripture:

But strong meat belongeth to them that are of full age, even those who by reason of use have their senses exercised to discern both good and evil.
- Hebrews 5:14 (KJV)

Caleb, like a dog, had the scent of the Promised Land in his spirit. Because of that scent, he kept himself fit for his future.

> *And now, behold, the LORD hath kept me alive, as he said, these forty and five years, even since the LORD spake this word unto Moses, while the children of Israel wandered in the wilderness: and now, lo, I am this day fourscore and five years old. As yet I am as strong this day as I was in the day that Moses sent me: as my strength was then, even so is my strength now, for war, both to go out, and to come in.*
> *- Joshua 14:10-11 (KJV)*

So what was so different about Caleb? You see, the others had good names, but except for Joshua, they were all void of true identity. Caleb, who had a name that others might not want, had his inheritance solidified in his spirit, and nothing, not even time itself, was going to stop this man who knew he was "well able."

CHOOSE YE THIS DAY

> *And if it seem evil unto you to serve the LORD, choose you this day whom ye will serve; whether the gods which your fathers served that were on the other side of the flood, or the gods of the Amorites, in whose land ye dwell: but as for me and my house, we will serve the LORD.*
> *- Joshua 24:15 (KJV)*

> *And all the congregation lifted up their voice, and cried; and the people wept that night. And all the children of Israel murmured against*

*Moses and against Aaron: and the whole
congregation said unto them,
Would God that we had died in the land of Egypt!
or would God we had died in this wilderness!
And wherefore hath the LORD brought us unto this
land, to fall by the sword, that our wives and our
children should be a prey? were it not better
for us to return into Egypt?
And they said one to another, Let us make a captain,
and let us return into Egypt.
- Numbers 14:1-4 (KJV)*

Read this scripture closely. It is speaking of the reaction
of the "fearful," those who are too full of fear to go in and
possess their God-given inheritance. There are four things I
notice in the above Scripture. First, fearful people are given
to depression. Depressed people do not sleep at night. Many
will lie awake tonight knowing that "There's got to be more
to life than this. God has a plan for me, but why do others
prosper and I can't even get by?" They will toss and turn in
turmoil over their future because they are simply too afraid.
They see everything as big as a giant, and see themselves as
too small and insignificant to conquer anything. They
continue to lose sleep night after night until they convince
themselves that all hope is lost.

Secondly, the fearful become persuaded that it would be
better to die in the wilderness than to face any obstacles in
pursuit of something better. These people live out their lives
in what I call chronic crisis.

Third, the fearful never want to draw closer to their
destiny. Rather, they always want to retreat. These people
will usually spend more time speaking of the past, because
they are too afraid of the future. I can clearly see in the
Scripture that we are not to be those who draw back.

Finally, the fearful will eventually speak against leadership. That preacher who is always telling them about the benefits of tithing will get on their bad side. They will begin to pass judgment on the very one who watches over their soul. If they were given the same opportunity King David had, they probably would have killed Saul. But David, who was not given to fear, said that he would not touch God's anointed. Even if your leader is wrong in something, have enough faith to allow God to deal with his heart.

And Joshua the son of Nun, and Caleb the son of
Jephunneh, which were of them that searched
the land, rent their clothes:
And they spake unto all the company of the children
of Israel, saying, The land, which we passed
through to search it, is an exceeding good land.
If the LORD delight in us, then he will bring us into
this land, and give it us; a land which
floweth with milk and honey.
Only rebel not ye against the LORD, neither fear ye
the people of the land; for they are bread for us:
their defence is departed from them, and the LORD
is with us: fear them not.
- Numbers 14:6-9 (KJV)

There are some things I've noticed about the faithful. First, they look at the land, not at the giants. Joshua and Caleb reported that the land was exceedingly good. So is the land that God has set before you. Sure there are obstacles and difficulties to overcome, but isn't every good thing worth a good fight?

The faithful will see themselves as the Lord's delight, despite failures, and even, at times, issues with sin. Because they are the Lord's delight, they know He will bring them into their land. God did not just get you out of bondage. He wants to bring you into abundance.

The faithful also refuse to rebel against God. While other spies and the rest of the Israelites rebelled against their earthly leaders, Joshua and Caleb were more interested in submitting to God.

Finally, the faithful are not given to fear. Did you know the phrase "fear not" is mentioned in the Bible 365 times? That means you could face a new giant every day of the year and you still would not have to accept the spirit of fear. You will overcome all your giants with love, power, and soundness of mind.

For God hath not given us the spirit of fear; but of
power, and of love, and of sound mind.
- II Timothy 1:7 (KJV)

I will be fruitful and multiply,
And my seed shall be great.
He will establish His covenant
As I trust in Him and wait.

8 WINNING IN THE REALM OF DIVINE PURPOSE

In previous chapters, we looked at the lives of Joseph, Caleb, and Joshua. These men had undeniable ability to hold on to their God-given promises until the appointed time of fulfillment. Again, we can see how the spirit of a true conqueror was demonstrated by Joseph. Despite all of the difficulty, his dream never died. No matter what kind of place or circumstance he found himself, his destiny as a ruler could not be denied. Regardless of his position, he always did more than survive. I believe his spirit was always saying something like: "Why should I simply survive when I've been called to supervise?" Even when he was a slave, God caused everything he did to prosper in his hand (Genesis 39:2-4). If you want to win the race that's been set before you, then you will need to live your life in the realm of divine purpose. We will enter into such a realm when we listen to the voice of the ruler within.

So God created man in his own image,
in the image of God created he him;
male and female created he them.
And God blessed them, and God said unto them,
Be fruitful, and multiply, and replenish the earth,
and subdue it: and have dominion over the fish of
the sea, and over the fowl of the air,
and over every living thing that moveth
upon the earth.
- Genesis 1:27-28 (KJV)

God has given each one of us the same mandate He gave to Adam. He's called us to be rulers. As rulers, we are to be fruitful and multiply, and we must have dominion in the earth. The Word of God empowers us to be partakers of His divine nature, and it is His nature to rule. We enter the realm of divine purpose when we believe God's Word, regardless of circumstance. All things are possible to those who believe. To believe is the same as agreeing with God. The Bible says there's power in agreement, so agreement with God releases His anointing. The anointing is burden-lifting, yoke destroying power. It's the ability to hold on to your God-given dream, even in the pit or the prison. The anointing never depends on circumstance. Spiritually speaking, what God has purposed within Himself has been set in stone long before your circumstance came to be. Like the Word of God, your destiny has been forever settled in heaven. It's up to you to get it established in the earth. In God, you have a destiny that cannot be denied. It's time to stop just surviving, and use the Word and the Spirit of God to begin thriving.

Now let's again consider Joshua, who also had the Spirit of a true conqueror. He had already been to his destination (Numbers 14:6-9). He knew it was a good land, and he knew God would delight in giving it to them. He also knew God had given him the ability to move forward without fear. How does this relate to us? God is trying to show us that to live in the realm of divine purpose, you will need to become like spies in the spirit realm. Those who will hear His words and believe them, and walk in the spirit, will begin to spy out their God-given inheritance. They will begin to see beyond today.

This book of the law shall not depart out of thy mouth; but thou shalt meditate therein day and night, that thou mayest observe to do according to all that is written therein: for then thou shalt make thy way prosperous, and then thou shalt have good

*success. Have not I commanded thee? Be strong
and of a good courage; be not afraid, neither be
thou dismayed: for the LORD thy God
is with thee whithersoever thou goest.*
- Joshua 1:8-9 (KJV)

Joshua's success is attributed to his consecration. He consecrated himself to speaking the Word of God. King David also asked God to set a guard about his mouth, so that he would not transgress against Him. To speak anything that is contrary to the Word is to sin against God.

*Keep your tongue from evil and your lips
from speaking deceit.*
- Psalm 34:13 (AMP)

Anything that contradicts the word of God is a lie. Those who are consecrated unto God will keep their tongues from speaking lies. Joshua also had an excellent spirit because he never hindered himself with procrastination. He understood the times. Once God's servant Moses died, as well as the rebellious generation who refused to go into the Promised Land, it was high time to get up and go forward.

God also wants *us* to discern the times. Once God does His part and opens up a door of opportunity, we must then do our part and walk through that door. If we don't, we have no right to cry to God or to blame the devil. If we want to live in the realm of divine purpose, then we must not hinder ourselves by procrastinating. We must be like Joshua and get up at once and possess our God-given promises. Now let's look at Jeremiah...

MORE THAN A WEEPING PROPHET

There are three things to consider regarding Jeremiah.

First, he had to overcome his own insecurities. Second, he conquered all obstacles through divine certainties. Finally, he became an expression of God's absolute ability. He was more than a weeping prophet. He was a man who lived in the realm of divine purpose.

STOP SPEAKING OF YOUR INSUFFICIENCIES

God knew in advance what kind of excuses Jeremiah would come up with, so He began to cover His bases. He clearly tells this young man that regardless of his age and opinion of himself, he has been pre-approved, pre-ordained, and pre-appointed. The Word of God came to Jeremiah to announce his life's assignment: to be a prophet to the nations. The response he gives is much like the response Moses gave God when he was called to be Israel's deliverer. In Exodus 4:10 and 6:12 Moses tries to explain his insufficiencies, "But God, I can't be a deliverer. I'm not eloquent, and they will never listen to me anyway."

Now therefore go, and I will be with thy mouth,
and teach thee what thou shalt say.
- Exodus 4:12 (KJV)

Thank God that He always goes with those He sends. He is with our mouths. Apart from Him, our mouths would get us into a lot of trouble. By His Spirit He will teach us just what to say and how to say it.

Back to Jeremiah's response, "Behold I cannot speak, for I am only a child." As if God didn't know this. God, in His infinite grace, has the answer, "Say not I am only a child."

Remember Joshua, he had to make sure God's Word never departed out of his mouth. The moment His words depart from your mouth, then words of insufficiency enter your speech. As a prophet to the nations, Jeremiah had to begin to agree with God. As stated before, agreement with God releases the anointing. Jeremiah had to start saying things like, "I will go wherever God sends me" and, "Whatever He commands, me to say, I'll say, I will not be afraid." After God dealt with the insecurity issues, He put forth His hand and touched his mouth.

But what saith it? The word is nigh thee,
even in thy mouth, and in thy heart: that is,
the word of faith, which we preach
- Romans 10:8 (KJV)

If we would become aware of the nearness of the most powerful thing on earth, the Word of God, then we would quickly begin to shake our own insecurities. We would soon be living in the realm of divine purpose. God's response to our long list of excuses is, "Speak not of your insufficiencies. My Word in you will cure you of all your insecurities."

CONQUERING ALL OBSTACLES

See, I have this day set thee over the nations and
over the kingdoms, to root out, and to pull down,
and to destroy, and to throw down,
to build, and to plant.
- Jeremiah 1:10 (KJV)

What we're seeing through Jeremiah's call is that we've all bee pre-approved, pre-ordained, and pre-appointed by God to do precisely what He's called us to do. He knows the obstacles that are before us, but we have some divine certainties to rely on. His Word in our mouth has the power over everything standing in opposition against us. Some obstacles have taken root many years before we were even born. Perhaps there are certain issues that have been evident in your family, neighborhood, or nation, for generations. As believers, we are anointed to root out anything that is contrary to the Gospel. Even if it is as strong as a generational curse, from the moment you were saved you had the ability to say, "The curse stops here!" The blood of Jesus not only had the power to wash away all your sin, but it also renders the effects of any generational sin powerless and ineffective, once and for all. The living Word in you has equipped you to root out any lie, whether that lie resides in you as an individual, or even that which may be deeply rooted in the nations. Like Jeremiah, we also have the ability to pull down strongholds.

> *For the weapons of our warfare are not carnal,*
> *but mighty through God to the pulling*
> *down of strongholds.*
> *- II Corinthians 4:10 (KJV)*

Sometimes the obstacles are so strong they're like a mighty fortress. What are we to do when we run up against one of these walls? We use our God-given weaponry, which is primarily the spoken Word of God, and our walk in the spirit. Our walk in the spirit is so important in pulling down strongholds. If you are exercising your spiritual senses, then you can hear the voice of discernment, which will direct you in dealing with these obstacles. If you fail to walk in the spirit, then strongholds will remain until you forsake all efforts of the flesh.

DESTINED TO DESTROY DEMONIC WORKS

When we as believers begin to allow the Word to dwell richly in us, the fruit of that Word will root out even that which has been around for generations. When we actively use our God-given weapons to pull down strongholds, then the works of the devil will be destroyed. We must become enforcers of kingdom rule. The Bible tells us that for this reason the Son of God was manifest, to destroy the works of the devil. Jesus had all the anointing that was needed to discern the devil, and to render him powerless. All he has left is the ability to deceive. I've often told believers that the moment you receive a lie as a reality, then you've empowered the devil to defeat you, at least for a season. But when you are able to discern demonic deception, then you're equipped to enforce kingdom rule and destroy the works of darkness.

But as for you, the anointing (the sacred appointment, the unction) which you received from Him abides [permanently] in you; [so] then you have no need that anyone should instruct you. But just as His anointing teaches you concerning every-thing and is true and is no falsehood, so you must abide in (live in, never depart from) Him [being rooted in Him, knit to Him], just as [His anointing] has taught you [to do].
- I John 2:27 (AMP)

Just as Jeremiah was anointed as a prophet, you are also anointed. You have the sacred appointment and the unction, which is the ability of the spirit abiding within you. This abiding anointing will teach you just how to deal with every obstacle. Jesus abiding in you is the Anointed One. The devil erected a cross as an obstacle against Christ. But death itself was defeated, as He rose from the dead. If the same spirit that raised Christ from the dead dwells in you, then why should you have any doubt about your God-given ability to eliminate all obstacles?

An Expression Of Absolute Ability

I've seen this illustration recently: an audience was asked, "How many believe that God can do anything?" The response was 100% yes. But when the same audience was asked, "How many believe that God could use *you*," only a small percentage actually believed God could use them as conduits of His power.

If a man therefore purge himself from these, he shall
be a vessel unto honour, sanctified, and meet for the
master's use, and prepared unto every good work.
- II Timothy 2:21 (KJV)

Vessels unto honor are like the prophet Jeremiah. They are well prepared and useful for any work of God. The following scripture speaks of God's absolute ability. It also shows us His ultimate goal for our lives. As it was for Israel, it is also for today's believers. God wants to satisfy those who are running to win with His goodness.

Hear the word of the LORD, O ye nations, and
declare it in the isles afar off, and say,
He that scattered Israel will gather him, and keep
him, as a shepherd doth his flock.
For the LORD hath redeemed Jacob, and ransomed
him from the hand of him that was stronger than he.
Therefore they shall come and sing in the height of
Zion, and shall flow together to the goodness of the
LORD, for wheat, and for wine, and for oil, and for
the young of the flock and of the herd: and their
soul shall be as a watered garden; and they shall
not sorrow any more at all.
Then shall the virgin rejoice in the dance, both
young men and old together: for I will turn their

*mourning into joy, and will comfort them, and make
them rejoice from their sorrow.
And I will satiate the soul of the priests with fatness,
and my people shall be satisfied with my goodness,
saith the LORD.*
- Jeremiah 31:10-14 (KJV)

First of all, Jesus is the Good Shepherd Who is able to gather His own. Just as He goes with those He sends, He also keeps them, wherever they go. The Bible says that His sheep know His voice, and the voice of His Spirit is ever-speaking. He shares His ways to enable you to shake all your insufficiencies.

Any insecurities you have come from your enemy. Apart from God, you were no match for the devil. But thank God, through Jesus, we've been redeemed from the hand of the enemy. We now have all power and authority over him.

We have reason enough to rejoice. We should ever be singing new songs of praise unto our God. In His goodness, He displayed His power. Our rejoicing and singing are expressions of His absolute ability to deliver us.

EVERY NEED IS MET

*But my God shall supply all your need
according to his riches in glory by Christ Jesus.*
- Philippians 4:19 (KJV)

So many of God's redeemed will not move forward for fear of lacking a natural need. God knows you have more than spiritual needs. So, through Christ, every emotional and physical need is already provided for. We should be such expressions of His goodness that our lives would be as fruitful fields, that anyone lacking could just come and glean from our well-watered gardens.

God's absolute ability turns mourning into joy. This is what we've been pre-approved, pre-ordained, and pre-appointed for.

WHAT IS THE SPIRIT SAYING?

What God said to the insecure prophet then, He says to the Church today. Regardless of opinions, obstacles, or demonic opposition, He's called us to be expressions of His ability. It's time to start running with complete confidence. Winners will always have to overcome the opinions of others. If you intend to win, you will need to remember this: you will never be fully aware of the power within you if you're preoccupied with the opinions of others.

Regarding obstacles, God's purpose in every stronghold is for you to realize you have the power to pull it down, while the demonic purpose of all opposition is to make you afraid. The prophet Elijah ran in fear of Jezebel's opposition. He ran all the way to a "cave of confrontation" with God, because he was intimidated. Because of the Word of the Lord, which is in our mouths, we don't have to run in fear. We are to run in faith, believing we've been pre-appointed as winners to live in the realm of divine purpose.

There's an appointed time for the promise,
And it will be fulfilled.
What matters most
Is that I run with patience, and yield.

9 RUNNING TOWARD PROMOTION

That ye be not slothful, but followers of them who
through faith and patience inherit the promises.
For when God made promise to Abraham, because
he could swear by no greater, he sware by himself,
Saying, Surely blessing I will bless thee,
and multiplying I will multiply thee.
And so, after he had patiently endured,
he obtained the promise.
- Hebrews 6:12-15 (KJV)

The heroes of faith in Hebrews chapter eleven would have never obtained their promises if they had not run in faith and patience. Before they could receive their rewards, they had to endure many tests. The problem in contemporary Christianity is that we want to enjoy the promise, without enduring the process. There is so much wisdom in the lives of the Old Testament prophets. One of my favorite men of God is Daniel. In the first two chapters of the book of Daniel, we can clearly see some power principles he used along the pathway to his promotion.

Power Principle #1 – Preparation

And the king spake unto Ashpenaz the master of his
eunuchs, that he should bring certain of the children
of Israel, and of the king's seed, and of the princes;
Children in whom was no blemish, but well

*favoured, and skilful in all wisdom, and cunning in
knowledge, and understanding science, and such as
had ability in them to stand in the king's palace,
and whom they might teach the learning and the
tongue of the Chaldeans.*
- Daniel 1:3-4 (KJV)

Daniel was among the young men selected to be
educated and well fed with the rich foods and wine from the
king's table. Daniel and his friends were chosen because
they were well prepared. God never sends promotion to the
unprepared.

First, they were prepared in their appearance. It's amaz-
ing, as well as disturbing, to see so many believers today
neglecting their own bodies, and putting little or no effort
into their personal appearance or health. It's as if to say that
because we are spiritual beings, we really don't need to pay
attention to physical health. Many will abuse their bodies in
disobedience to Scripture, which tells us we are the temple
of the Holy Ghost. Later, when disease shows up in our
bodies, we beg God to heal us. Thank God for His mercy,
but when will we begin to take this issue seriously? For
some of us, it's a challenge, but nonetheless, it is of great
importance. We as believers must become mindful of our
health and appearance.

Of course, I'm not speaking of perfection. That usually
leads to obsession, but we do make an impression with the
way we look. So at any age and any weight, we should look
our best. Just as Jesus was the express image of God, we are
now His express image in the earth. I cannot imagine Jesus
neglecting His appearance or His health, so why should we
neglect ours?

For the earnest expectation of the creature waiteth
for the manifestation of the sons of God.
- Romans 8:19 (KJV)

All the earth is yearning to see the manifestation of the sons of God. The natural man cannot receive spiritual things. Unbelievers can only see you in the natural sense. For this reason, we the Church should find ways to stand up and stick out. God's people should be the best looking and the healthiest people on earth. After all, we are here to be His witnesses.

Get wisdom, get understanding: forget it not;
neither decline from the words of my mouth.
Forsake her not, and she shall preserve thee:
love her, and she shall keep thee.
Wisdom is the principal thing; therefore get
wisdom: and with all thy getting get understanding.
- Proverbs 4:5-7 (KJV)

Secondly, Daniel and his friends were well prepared in godly wisdom. Wisdom is the principle thing. Wherever you are, even in a land of captivity, wisdom will promote you if you embrace her.

If any of you is deficient in wisdom, let him ask of
the giving God [Who gives] to everyone liberally
and ungrudgingly, without reproaching or faultfind-
ing, and it will be given him.
- James 1:5 (AMP)

Many times, God's people are not promoted because they lack wisdom. They are deficient in knowledge and understanding. So often we're lacking, but never asking. Or, when we ask, we waver. If you ask in faith believing to receive, He won't start looking for some fault that would disqualify you. God shows no partiality to His people.

> *And that from childhood you have known the Holy*
> *Scriptures, which are able to make you wise for salvation*
> *through faith which is in Christ Jesus.*
> *- II Timothy 3:15 (KJV)*

We must also go beyond just asking God for wisdom, and become students of His Word. We must study to show ourselves approved, as workmen that are without shame. You will never outgrow your need for learning scriptural principles. The "school of the spirit" is one from which we should never wish to graduate. The Bible says that wise men will continue to increase in knowledge and understanding. The moment you begin to think you've arrived, that you've learned all there is to learn, you've just stopped short of your next God-given promotion.

> *Reprove not a scorner, lest he hate you;*
> *reprove a wise man, and he will love you.*
> *Give instruction to a wise man and he will be yet*
> *wiser; teach a righteous man (one upright and in*
> *right standing with God) and he will increase in*
> *learning. The reverent and worshipful fear of the*
> *Lord is the beginning (the chief and choice part) of*
> *Wisdom, and the knowledge of the Holy one is*
> *insight and understanding. For by me [Wisdom from*
> *God] your days shall be multiplied, and the years of*
> *your life shall be increased. If you are wise, you are*
> *wise for yourself; if you scorn, you alone*
> *will bear it and pay the penalty.*
> *- Proverbs 9:8-12 (AMP)*

On the pathway to promotion, there will be times when

we'll need to receive a reproof or two, and perhaps some words of instruction from those who have more wisdom than we do. If we receive their words with a right spirit, then we will increase in understanding. On the other hand, if we resist words of wisdom, we'll lose opportunity to learn life's valuable lessons.

Proverbs 9:10 speaks of the fear of the Lord. A wise man will increase in knowledge and understanding because he fears the Lord. He will gladly receive wise counsel, which will cause him to increase. The fear of the Lord is the spirit of true humility. Those who fear the Lord, and are clothed in humility, will continue to increase in learning. Promotion is prepared for the one who will not give pride a place in their lives.

Preparation is a principle that is resisted by many believers. We've been so influenced by the society we live in, that we expect promotion to come instantly. It may come suddenly for those who have made themselves ready, but it never comes for the unprepared. There's no better time than the present to begin to embrace the process and become prepared for the coming promotion. Let's, consider the following:

- No water for the army, until the ditches were dug (II Kings 3:16)
- No oil until vessels were gathered (II Kings 4:3-4)
- No healing for lepers until they dipped seven times (II Kings 5:10)
- No Messiah until the way had been prepared (Isaiah 40:3)
- No harvest until the ground had been broken (Hosea 10:12)
- No vision without obedience (John 9:7)
- No resurrection until the stone had been removed (John 11:39)

Power Principle #2 – Purpose to be Pure

> *But Daniel determined in his heart that he would
> not defile himself by [eating his portion of] the
> king's rich and dainty food or by [drinking] the
> wine which he drank; therefore he requested of the
> chief of the eunuchs that he might [be allowed] not
> to defile himself. Now God made Daniel to find
> favor, compassion, and loving-kindness with
> the chief of the eunuchs.*
> *- Daniel 1:8-9 (AMP)*

To Daniel, eating of the king's portion would have
defiled him, so he determined not to. He had higher expecta-
tions for his life, therefore he purposed to keep himself
pure. He may have been living in captivity, but on the inside
he enjoyed true liberty. His food choices were not about his
preference, but about his conviction. To have the ability to
remain pure in heart, no matter where you are, is true
liberty. And believe it or not, purity can actually set you up
for favor.

> *So whoever cleanses himself [from what is
> ignoble and unclean, who separates himself
> from contact with contaminating and
> corrupting influences] will [then himself] be
> a vessel set apart and useful for honorable
> and noble purposes, consecrated and
> profitable to the Master, fit and ready
> for any good work.*
> *- II Timothy 2:21 (AMP)*

Daniel was a man set apart for God. He kept himself
from contact with contaminating and corrupt influences. At
that time, he may not have known exactly how the Lord

planned to use his life, but he did see himself as a vessel set apart for God. Even in a difficult place, God had noble and honorable purposes for him, so Daniel wanted to be ready for any good work. One of the greatest promotions we could ever receive is the privilege of being used by God. He uses those who keep themselves pure and undefiled.

In today's world, even adults will encounter "peer pressure." We all know what this is. It's when your peers put pressure on you to do something that may not please the Lord. This pressure has the potential to short-circuit your next promotion.

If you want to be a vessel unto honor, you will have to become willing to run the risk of being different. As it was for Daniel, so it will be for you. If you run the risk of being different because of your convictions, then you will ultimately win the respect of others.

Just as Joseph found favor with the governor, so Daniel found favor with the chief of the eunuchs. I believe this happened for these two men because they had the conviction to walk in their integrity. The Bible says that integrity will preserve you. Both men were preserved in places of captivity because of their pure hearts. God always preserves those He plans to promote. If you've ever wondered why the difficulties of your life have not consumed you, it is because the Lord has plans to promote you. If you will begin to agree with God's plan, you will keep yourself pure and ready for His use.

Power Principle #3 – Procure an Audience With the King

> *Then Daniel went in, and desired of the king that he*
> *would give him time, and that he would shew the*
> *king the interpretation.*
> *- Daniel 2:16 (KJV)*

The king had a problem, and Daniel was God's man to solve it. What a change that would take place in the world if every time our authorities had a problem, we would see ourselves as God's servants to solve them.

The king had dreams that troubled his spirit, and he was losing sleep. But his problem became Daniel's opportunity. Look at the confidence he displays before the king; consider his fearlessness and boldness. Keep in mind that no one had ever been told just what was seen in the dream. The king was looking for the one who could both see the dream and interpret it's meaning. No king had ever made such a request; it was impossible. Praise God, what is impossible with man, is possible with God's man, but only for the one who uses the opportunity to show off his God. Daniel's decision to do this would save his life, as well as the lives of others.

> *For this cause the king was angry and very furious,*
> *and commanded to destroy all the*
> *wise men of Babylon.*
> *- Daniel 2:12 (KJV)*

In the face of death itself, Daniel would boldly make his reservation to show the king what God could do. At this time, he did not have a revelation on the matter, but he did have some perception. Daniel perceived that if he would secure time with the king, God would make known the dream and it's interpretation. By now you should be able to see the progression. If you're well prepared in wisdom and appearance, inside and out, and you keep your life pure, then God will bring you before kings. Would to God, more believers had this kind of faith.

We need to become more like Daniel, and see the problems that are in our places of employment as opportunities. This may be a key to our promotion. Even if you don't have the answer today, you can begin by calling those things that are not as though they are. God has a plan to promote those who will operate with spiritual perception.

Power Principle #4 – Prayer of Agreement

> *Then Daniel went to his house, and made the thing*
> *known to Hananiah, Mishael, and Azariah, his*
> *companions: That they would desire mercies of the*
> *God of heaven concerning this secret; that Daniel*
> *and his fellows should not perish with the*
> *rest of the wise men of Babylon.*
> *- Daniel 2:17-18 (KJV)*

> *Again I say unto you, That if two of you shall agree*
> *on earth as touching any thing that they shall ask, it*
> *shall be done for them of my Father which is in*
> *heaven. For where two or three are gathered*
> *together in my name, there am I*
> *in the midst of them.*
> *- Matthew 18:19 (KJV)*

The above two scriptures illustrate the power that's in the prayer of agreement. Whenever there is a crisis, we should have at least one Christian companion that we can get into agreement with. It's sad to say, but united prayer is a privilege that is neglected by many believers. The Bible tells us to bear one another's burdens. I have a friend who is a senior pastor of an inner city work, where there are multitudes of needs. Yet, he is always fasting and praying for someone else's breakthrough. He is the kind of person who will always take the time to listen, and to pray. We all need people like this in our lives. We also need to be people who are never too preoccupied with our own issues to pray with a friend in need. Many in the Body of Christ are bearing heavy burdens. Again, it's so sad to say that they bear their burdens alone. The Bible also says to rejoice with those who rejoice, but I have found that when believers don't join others in prayer, they are not all that moved when someone else receives their breakthrough. I've often asked God why the contemporary Christian world is not seeing more miracles, like in the New Testament church.

> *And they continued stedfastly in the apostles'*
> *doctrine and fellowship, and in breaking of bread,*
> *and in prayers. And fear came upon every soul: and*
> *many wonders and signs were done by the apostles.*
> *- Acts 2:42 (KJV)*

I believe more wonders and signs will be performed through us when we return, not only to sound doctrine, but to united prayer and true fellowship. It is time to spend more time and effort praying together, bearing one another's burdens, and rejoicing over one another's victories.

When Daniel and his friends prayed, they requested God's mercy. Remember, Daniel stepped out in faith and had made his appointment to interpret the dream. They needed mercy to manifest, or they would lose their lives. Simply put, mercy met the need.

> *Then was the secret revealed unto Daniel in a night*
> *vision. Then Daniel blessed the God of heaven.*
> *- Daniel 2:19 (KJV)*

Mercy met the need in the night. Many times this is how God works in the midst of a serious need. They were looking at a "do or die" situation. Either God was going to do something (which was to reveal the secret), or they were going to die. Well, God did do something. He showed up in a vision in the night to reveal the secret to Daniel.

And it shall come to pass afterward, that I will pour out my spirit upon all flesh; and your sons and your daughters shall prophesy, your old men shall dream dreams, your young men shall see visions:
- Joel 2:28-29 (KJV)

Daniel lived in a day when God revealed His will and way through divine visitation. For example, some would have dreams, see visions, or encounter angelic visitors, while others would hear the audible voice of God. There were various ways God would manifest Himself to His people. But that was the Old Testament. We are New Testament believers, who have the Holy Spirit abiding in us. How much more should we see signs of God's supernatural ability? I believe that there are miracles waiting for those who would make more effort in praying the prayer of agreement. Promotion is prepared for those who will pray!

Power Principle #5 – Praise Him

Daniel answered and said, Blessed be the name of God for ever and ever: for wisdom and might are his
- Daniel 2:20 (KJV)

One of the missing elements in prayer in today's Church is praise. Often we're caught up in ourselves, and we forget to praise the One Who meets our need. Praise also expresses what we are expecting God to do for us.

And when they began to sing and to praise, the LORD set ambushments against the children of Ammon, Moab, and mount Seir, which were come against Judah; and they were smitten.
For the children of Ammon and Moab stood up

against the inhabitants of mount Seir, utterly to slay
and destroy them: and when they had made an end
of the inhabitants of Seir, every one helped
to destroy another.
And when Judah came toward the watch tower in
the wilderness, they looked unto the multitude, and,
behold, they were dead bodies fallen to the earth,
and none escaped.
- II Chronicles 20:22-24 (KJV)

There is power in your praise. If you only knew what was taking place in the spiritual realm, you would be more aggressive in it. So put your praise on; when you do, God creates confusion, division, and disorder for your enemy.

Let the high praises of God be in their mouth, and a
twoedged sword in their hand;
- Psalm 149:6 (KJV)

God uses the high praise, which is the praise of expectation, to execute vengeance upon your enemy. Prayer is wonderful, but prayer alone is not enough. We should seal every prayer with praise. Daniel declared that wisdom and might were God's. He shared a word of wisdom with Daniel. This gift of the spirit was used to demonstrate God's might.

Power Principle #6 – Proclaim God's Ability

And he changeth the times and the seasons: he
removeth kings, and setteth up kings: he giveth
wisdom unto the wise, and knowledge to them that
know understanding:
- Daniel 2:21 (KJV)

God can change a season suddenly, and He can even use

you to do it. He can set someone up as a king, yet he can set another down just as quickly. He doesn't ask for anyone's permission to do anything.

Now that we've proclaimed His ability, let's talk about *our* abilities. Obstacles are our opportunities, and disappointments are our appointments. If you're faced with obstacles, then be wise enough to ask God for wisdom. If you're disappointed, then see it as God's appointment to bring a change. God is able to do something great in your situation, and He's looking to use you to do it.

> *He reveals deep and secret things;*
> *He knows what is in the darkness,*
> *And light dwells with Him.*
> *- Daniel 2:22 (KJV)*

Power Principle #7 – Pursue Good

> *Therefore Daniel went to Arioch, whom the king*
> *had appointed to destroy the wise men of Babylon.*
> *He went and said thus to him: "Do not destroy the*
> *wise men of Babylon; take me before the king, and I*
> *will tell the king the interpretation."*
> *- Daniel 2:24 (KJV)*

> *And of some have compassion, making a difference.*
> *- Jude 22 (KJV)*

What an act of compassion! We would probably have thought, "good riddance," and allowed the magicians, astrologers, and Chaldeans to be put to death. But Daniel was a man who, having compassion, made the difference. This in itself was an act of wisdom. As God would have it, those who were spared from death would later submit themselves to

Daniel's leadership (Daniel 2:48).

Power Principle #8 – Partakers of His Divine Nature

> *Daniel answered in the presence of the king, and*
> *said, The secret which the king hath demanded*
> *cannot the wise men, the astrologers, the magicians,*
> *the soothsayers, shew unto the king;*
> *But there is a God in heaven that revealeth secrets,*
> *and maketh known to the king Nebuchadnezzar*
> *what shall be in the latter days. Thy dream, and the*
> *visions of thy head upon thy bed, are these;*
> *As for thee, O king, thy thoughts came into thy mind*
> *upon thy bed, what should come to pass hereafter:*
> *and he that revealeth secrets maketh known to thee*
> *what shall come to pass.*
> *- Daniel 2:27-29 (KJV)*

Ultimately, God wants to put His people in circumstances that demand an answer. The answer is hidden, and cannot be discovered by any amount of human effort. It is God's nature to know things that man cannot know, but that men and women of God can know. He's looking for someone who would become a partaker of His divine nature. There are promises for promotion for all of God's people. These promises are found in the Word of God, which will make you wise enough to stand before kings.

> *Whereby are given unto us exceeding great and*
> *precious promises: that by these ye might be partak-*
> *ers of the divine nature,*
> *- II Peter 1:4 (KJV)*

Power Principle #9 – Promotion Means Process

All wise runners will realize there is a process. We must embrace and endure the process so we can enjoy the promises. God wants to use us, along the pathway to promotion. He uses those whose hearts and lives are well prepared, purified, and set apart for His purpose. These are people who have the courage to call things that are not as though they are. They always turn trouble into triumph. The men and women of God who will pray, seal every prayer with praise, and seek to do good, will become the partakers of God's divine nature.

As stated in the opening scripture of this chapter, *"Be not slothful, but followers of those who through faith and patience inherit the promises."*

I'll yield to the One
Who's called me to run.
I've purposed in my heart
To glorify the Son.

10 Winning As A True Worshipper

Real winners will become true worshippers. The Bible tells us that God is seeking those who will worship Him in spirit and in truth. Most of us associate worship with bowing down and singing songs of adoration unto God. While these things are wonderful, true worship is so much more.

Immediate Obedience

When thou saidst, Seek ye my face; my heart said
unto thee, Thy face, LORD, will I seek.
- Psalm 27:8 (KJV)

What has been your response to God's call to seek His face? Has your heart said, "Your face Lord, will I seek?" We all have to face reality and become honest with ourselves, because God desires truth in our inward parts. The same spirit that spoke to David is speaking to us today. God is saying, "Seek My face."

Many have resisted this wonderful invitation to become seekers of God. If your heart has avoided the opportunity to respond correctly, then make a decision right where you are to become a true worshipper of God. True worship is immediate obedience.

And Abraham rose up early in the morning, and
saddled his ass, and took two of his young men with

him, and Isaac his son,
and clave the wood for the burnt offering, and rose
up, and went unto the place of which God had told
him. Then on the third day Abraham lifted up his
eyes, and saw the place afar off.
And Abraham said unto his young men, Abide ye
here with the ass; and I and the lad will go yonder
and worship, and come again to you
- Genesis 22:3-5 (KJV)

The above scripture is the first place in the Bible where the word "worship" is used. On the evening before, God had instructed Abraham to offer his only son as a sacrifice. So, early the next morning he prepared to obey God. Most of us would have argued with God, went to bed, and slept in the next morning. Not Abraham, he obeyed immediately. He was one of God's true worshippers. Without instruments and singers, worship was taking place.

LOOKING UP

Then on the third day Abraham lifted up his eyes,
and saw the place afar off.
And Abraham said unto his young men, Abide ye
here with the ass; and I and the lad will go yonder
and worship, and come again to you
- Genesis 22:4-5 (KJV)

On the third day, Abraham looked up and saw the place of worship in the distance. It was a three day journey to Mount Moriah. No one else knew the task that God had set before him.

Set your affection on things above,
not on things on the earth.
- Colossians 3:2 (KJV)

Abraham's affections were set, not on his son whom he loved deeply, but on his God. Not to make him out to be an uncaring father, but Abraham had to hold fast to the promise God had given him. Through his seed, all the earth would be blessed. Even in this, he continued to count God as faithful.

Looking away [from all that will distract] to Jesus,
Who is the Leader and the Source of our faith
[giving the first incentive for our belief] and is also
its Finisher [bringing it to maturity and perfection].
He, for the joy [of obtaining the prize] that was set
before Him, endured the cross, despising and ignor-
ing the shame, and is now seated at the right hand
of the throne of God.
- Hebrews 12:2 (AMP)

Abraham could not afford to allow himself to be distracted by his own emotional attachments to his son. Distractions will keep you from discerning the voice of God. He had to keep looking to the source of his faith, which was God. True worship is actively looking away from all distractions. Distractions have the ability to keep you from immediate obedience. Remember, delayed obedience is disobedience.

SEPARATION

And Abraham said unto his young men, Abide ye
here with the ass; and I and the lad will go yonder
and worship, and come again to you
- Genesis 22:5 (KJV)

Isolation leads to revelation, which is God revealing what man can not discover on his own. It is also the revealing of a reality that was previously not perceived.

Abraham was already abiding under the spirit of revelation when he declared, "We will worship, then we will come back to you." He must have known that even if Isaac was reduced to ashes, God would still raise him from the dead. So many today will avoid isolation or separation. They are satisfied with their busy lifestyle. There's plenty of church-going, fellowship, and joint Bible studies. Some are just surviving on information, but the apostle Paul prayed for the Church to have the spirit of revelation, not the spirit of information.

Jesus said that man cannot live by bread alone. Spiritually speaking, Christian information is likened to bread. Bread alone will never sustain your spirit man. The only thing that will satisfy your inner man is revelation, and again, revelation is reserved for those who will seek isolation and separation.

CASTING ALL CARES

And they came to the place which God had told him of; and Abraham built an altar there, and laid the wood in order, and bound Isaac his son, and laid him on the altar upon the wood.
- Genesis 22:9 (KJV)

Can you imagine the moment when Isaac asked about the sacrifice? Abraham's answer, "God will provide the lamb," proves he was a true worshipper. As believers, we know that God provided the ultimate Lamb of sacrifice, Jesus Christ. He secured the free gift of salvation for us. Many only see their salvation as a guaranteed reservation in heaven. But it's so much more. It is also preservation, deliverance, healing, soundness of mind, and prosperity. As you're giving heed to God's call to become a worshipper, keep the true meaning of salvation in mind. When you do, you will be able to cast every care upon the One Who cares for you.

> *Who shall ascend into the holy hill of the Lord? or*
> *who shall stand in his holy place?*
> *- Psalm 24:3 (KJV)*

As we ascend unto the holy hill of worship, let us drop off all the distractions. Many times the distractions are attacks (from the enemy), personal bondages, discomforts, any kind of lack, and turmoil in our minds. Again, God has provided a Lamb (Jesus Christ) Who has secured the free gift of salvation. So choose you this day. You can worry or you can worship.

HEARING THE VOICE OF HEAVEN

> *And they came to the place which God had*
> *told him of; and Abraham built an altar*
> *there, and laid the wood in order, and bound*
> *Isaac his son, and laid him on the altar*
> *upon the wood. And Abraham stretched*
> *forth his hand, and took the knife to slay his*
> *son. And the angel of the LORD called unto*
> *him out of heaven, and said, Abraham,*
> *Abraham: and he said, Here am I.*
> *- Genesis 22:9-11 (KJV)*

This worshipper went all the way. He did not stop short of doing exactly what God commanded him to do. Just as he took the knife to slay his son, he heard an angel call from heaven. Thank God he was able to hear that voice!

Worship is, and always has been, a two way experience.

Our part is to respond with immediate obedience, and God's part is to speak with the voice of provision. The voice of provision calls us by name. It will keep us from slaying the very seed God will use to bring the blessing to the earth.

GIVING GOD EVERYTHING

And he said, Lay not thine hand upon the lad,
neither do thou any thing unto him: for now I know
that thou fearest God, seeing thou hast not withheld
thy son, thine only son from me.
And Abraham lifted up his eyes, and looked, and
behold behind him a ram caught in a thicket by his
horns: and Abraham went and took the ram,
and offered him up for a burnt offering
in the stead of his son.
And Abraham called the name of that place
Jehovah-jireh: as it is said to this day, In the mount
of the LORD it shall be seen.
- Genesis 22:12-14 (KJV)

True worship is giving back to God what He has given to you. When you do this, it proves your fear of the Lord. Many say they fear God, but have no acts of obedience to prove it. Many want financial blessing, but they refuse to be obedient in tithing. Tithing is giving back to God the first fruit of your labors. It's more than an act of obedience; it's a privilege that really sets you up for increase. This was illustrated in my life last year when the Lord spoke to my husband and I about our first fruit offerings. He invited us to give my entire salary to the kingdom for the month of January, in addition to our regular tithe and offerings. We gave as an act of worship unto God. We gave with an expectation, not for gain, but to see God's will accomplished in our lives. Financial blessing came suddenly, within four months, and in four times the amount that was given. This was only one of many times God has proven to us that we can never out give Him. You can't lose with God's principles of giving. When you give God everything, not only will it come back to you in good measure, but it also sets you up to receive a fresh revelation of who God is.

And Abraham called the name of that place
Jehovah-jireh: as it is said to this day, In the mount
of the LORD it shall be seen.
- Genesis 22:14 (KJV)

Abraham knew that if God would spare Isaac, then His provision could be seen anywhere, at any time. He declared on the mountain of the Lord, "It will be provided." He is still Jehovah Jireh. His provision shall be seen on the mountain of worship.

THE FRUIT OF TRUE WORSHIP

And the angel of the LORD called unto Abraham
out of heaven the second time,
And said, By myself have I sworn, saith the LORD,
for because thou hast done this thing, and hast not
withheld thy son, thine only son:
That in blessing I will bless thee, and in multiplying
I will multiply thy seed as the stars of the heaven,
and as the sand which is upon the sea shore; and
thy seed shall possess the gate of his enemies.
And in thy seed shall all the nations of the earth be
blessed; because thou hast obeyed My voice.
- Genesis 22:15-18 (KJV)

We need to stay on the mountain of worship long enough to hear the second voice. The first voice was the voice of provision, while the second is the voice of blessing. This voice of blessing speaks of generational authority. We hear so much about generational curses, but here God is speaking of generational blessing. When God says, "In blessing, I will bless you," it means the blessing will increase with every generation. The blessing is the ability to possess the enemy's gate. The word "gate" here indicates all the strengths, whether troops, councils, or fortified cities, of the enemy. We possess the enemy's gate when we outnumber them.

The voice of blessing also speaks of supernatural influence to the nations.

> *I will declare the decree: the LORD hath said unto*
> *me, Thou art my Son; this day have I begotten thee.*
> *Ask of me, and I shall give thee the heathen for*
> *thine inheritance, and the uttermost parts of the*
> *earth for thy possession.*
> *- Psalm 2:7-8 (KJV)*

It may strike you as strange, but the potential of pure worship is in that the nations come to Christ. We cannot imagine God the Father withholding anything from His beloved Son. The Son asked His Father for nations. The highest form of worship, which is obedience, has the potential to usher in the knowledge of His glory for the nations.

Lastly, the voice of blessing speaks of the thousand-fold. Those who are willing to part with anything for God shall have it made up to them with manifold blessing. Abraham only had one son, and was willing to offer him as a sacrifice. God spared Isaac and rewarded Abraham's obedience by making him the father of millions.

> *And in thy seed shall all the nations of the earth be*
> *blessed; because thou hast obeyed my voice.*
> *So Abraham returned unto his young men, and they*

*rose up and went together to Beer-sheba; and
Abraham dwelt at Beer-sheba.
- Genesis 22:18-19 (KJV)*

It's time for the Church to rise up as winners. Real winners will count the cost and, without shame, obey God's call to be true worshippers. Once again, be honest with yourself. Today is the day to answer with your whole heart and say, "Your face Lord, will I seek."

I know there are many distractions and emotional attachments, but we're being called to look away from those things. The Author and Finisher is calling forth winners to set their affections on the things above. Separate yourself unto God. Don't be afraid of isolation. Out of it will come revelation. God wants to make mysteries known to you.

Trade in your worry for worship. God isn't out to hurt you or take from you. He doesn't want to withhold any good thing. Today we've been given the same privilege of hearing God's voice of provision, and His voice of blessing. Our part in all this is to give Him everything. When we do, we'll be met with a fresh revelation of who He really is. The byproduct of that relationship between the Church and her God is that nations will come to know Him.

So regardless of what others may say,
Regardless of what the enemy
may bring my way,
Regardless of setbacks through
failures or sin,
I've been chosen to run, and I'm
running to win!

11 RUNNING AS A WINNER

Every winner will have to develop the tenacity to overcome the opinions of others. Others will not always be there for you, and when they are, they still cannot be your main source of encouragement. Ultimately, God must be your source in all things. Because God's opinion matters most, always let what God says determine the way you should go.

Then there's the enemy, who is the thief. He comes only to steal, kill and destroy. When we rise up with a determination to win this Christian race, he will also rise up and attempt to afflict us. I like to say that every time the devil tries to afflict me, it will be turned around for my good. My victory always proves that my God is God, and He will never fail me. It's so important to live with a strong sense of destiny. When you do, the adversary, who comes to devour, will not be able to torment you with the spirit of fear.

One of the fears that come upon God's people is the fear of failure; the fear of making such a horrible mistake that we would never be able to recover. Or, that God is really holding our past sin against us. This is nothing more than condemnation, resulting in a sense of hopelessness and despair.

Condemnation is based on past sin or mistakes. The Bible says, *"There is now no condemnation to those who are in Christ Jesus."* The One Who is faithful and just is always willing and able to forgive any sin. His blood was shed once, and for all sin; past, present, and future. Regardless of the multitude of excuses we may come up with, God has chosen us to run this race, and has ordained us to win. It's a part of His infinite plan for our lives, which He established before the foundations of the earth. It's time to stop speaking of all of our insuffiencies. Begin to rely on God's grace, which is His divine ability operating freely in our lives.

OVERCOMING ALL OBSTACLES

He staggered not at the promise of God through
unbelief; but was strong in faith, giving glory to
God; And being fully persuaded that, what he had
promised, he was able also to perform.
- Roman 4:20-21 (KJV)

I've spent so many years of my life staggering at the promises of God. Wanting to believe them, yet being too weak in faith to conceive them as my own. Many times, I asked God why it was so difficult to believe, and to have child-like faith. I continue to thank Him for being both Father and Friend to me. As a Father, He would show me the way to go, and as a Friend, He would stay beside me, encouraging me along the way. When others began to voice their opinions, and disapprove of me, He would remind me of foundational truths, like, "I can do all things through Christ who strengthens me, I am an overcomer through Christ, and He has made me to be more than a conqueror." I had to make a decision to get into agreement with God, and to disagree with anything that is contrary to His will, His Word, or His way.

I don't like to go into great detail about demonic attack, because it wastes time that could be used to glorify God. I will just say that there have been many weapons formed against my family, as there are with any of God's servants. Praise God, the enemy has never succeeded in any of his plans to destroy us. Now that we have grandchildren that are showing signs of God's gifts and callings, it is easy to see why the devil would do anything he could to stop us from moving forward in God. He is after our seed. The Bible tells us that our seed will be great and will possess the enemy's gates. I'm sure this fact torments the devil to no end. When you are under demonic attack, you must put it in perspective. It's not always about you. It's really about what's coming from you, the fruit of your womb. That's why you (women) should call the fruit of your womb blessed. Regardless of what the enemy may say, you and your seed (natural and spiritual) are blessed.

So many times, I would think that the attack was about me, my calling, or my anointing. Now I know that it's beyond me. There will not be enough time in my life to fulfill all the dreams and visions God has given to me. The Word tells us that God will increase our families yet more and more. I'm glad that my children and grandchildren are increasing and becoming more than I've ever dreamed of. I can think of no greater joy on earth than to see all my dreams and visions accomplished through my seed.

Don't let the devil destroy your dreams. Don't let him tell you that you will never accomplish anything great in your life, or that you will never produce any fruit. Don't sell yourself short of seeing your seed increasing in the earth. God wants to use you and your children to establish His covenant. This is the most satisfying way to live our lives. Don't ever again let the devil tell you that God doesn't want you to win. God has pre-determined the course, and pre-ordained your steps. He's already seen the day you'll finish your race. He's looking forward to saying, "Well done, good and faithful servant."

I pray that learning these simple, yet proven principles has made you to feel empowered to become strong in faith, like our father Abraham. It certainly is time for the church to stop halting between opinions, and to stop staggering at the promises of God. Join me in becoming fully persuaded, and completely convinced that God, Who gave the promises in the first place, will also perform them. Remember that He never does anything apart from man. He seeks to use us as workmen together with Him to accomplish His will.

Don't let another day go by without recapturing those God-given dreams. It's not too late. You're not too old. God can still impregnate you with a promise. Greater faith will come to you through hearing the Word of God. You can become stronger in that faith every day. Even if your natural family has forsaken you, let God lift you up. There is a new dimension in God that's waiting to be discovered.

THE WINNERS PSALM

The LORD is my shepherd; I shall not want. He maketh me to lie down in green pastures: he leadeth me beside the still waters.
He restoreth my soul: he leadeth me in the paths of righteousness for his name's sake.
Yea, though I walk through the valley of the shadow of death, I will fear no evil: for thou art with me; thy rod and thy staff they comfort me. Thou preparest a table before me in the presence of mine enemies: thou anointest my head with oil; my cup runneth over. Surely goodness and mercy shall follow me all the days of my life: and I will dwell in the house of the LORD for ever.
- Psalm 23 (KJV)

You are not alone; the Good Shepherd is with you. He will always supply all your need, according to His riches in glory. David was a shepherd who was anointed to be king over Israel. His pathway for obtaining that promise was long and difficult, yet God met all of his spiritual, emotional, and physical needs. God will do the same for those who will keep Him in remembrance of His Word. Many times, we suffer lack just because we don't know, or believe, what the Word says about God supplying our need. Other times, it's because of our unwillingness to agree with what He says about our circumstances.

As a Good Shepherd, He will feed your spirit. The Word of God is substance to your spirit man. If your spirit is not strong, you will not have the needed endurance to stay in the race. You must continually have an ear to hear His words. Jesus said, "The words I speak are spirit and life."

He will also lead you into places of peace. How many times have we heard someone say, "If I could just find some peace and quiet?" There is something inside each one of us that is searching for perfect peace. The Word tells us to be still and know that He is God, but many times we're too busy running around, trying to find the answers to life's problems somewhere else. All the while God is calling us to the place of peace. It is there that our mind's can be renewed and our strength restored. The Spirit of The Lord taught me several years ago that the creative power of God can only flow through the one who is given over to His Spirit of perfect peace. This peace can only come to those whose minds are focused on the Lord.

The Spirit of God is our guide as we travel the pathway of righteousness. This pathway is not just some dull, dusty road that will someday lead us to heaven. No, it's a path that should be getting brighter with each passing day. One of the ways to make your path brighter is to understand that it is a path of righteousness. Along the way, we need to learn to recognize anything that is contrary to righteousness. The kingdom of God is righteousness, peace, and joy. We represent His kingdom in the earth. If you think about the kingdom of heaven, you will not imagine lack, sickness, or sadness of any kind. In teaching us how to pray, Jesus instructed us to say, "As it is in heaven, so let it be in the earth." So while we are in the earth, we can exercise our right to expect God's kingdom to manifest in our lives. As ambassadors of the kingdom, we should use our authority against anything that is not righteousness, peace, and joy.

There will be times of difficulty, and you may even experience the shadow of death at the passing of a loved one. At times, circumstances will scream that God is not with you. You may even feel forsaken; I know I have. You will need to see, whether you feel it or not, that the light of God's presence in your life is what creates the shadow during difficulty. During the most difficult times of my life, I would have been overcome with darkness, if it were not for the presence of the Lord. Not that I always feel His presence, sometimes I don't. But I have learned that we are not to walk by feelings. By faith, I know that the God of all comfort is ever with me. The truth of His Word has delivered me from all fear. I know that even when the enemy comes to devour me, he will stumble and fall.

God has a table prepared for us, even in the presence of our enemies. In spite of circumstances, God is still calling us to feed our spirit man, to feast at His table, and to continue to grow closer to Him.

One of the most difficult things to ever experience happened to a sister in the Lord, when she lost her husband to suicide. During the home going service, she stood before the Lord and worshipped Him in sign language. She was absolutely lost in God's presence. I remember thinking how she was feasting at God's table in the presence of her enemies. Nothing brings more glory to God than to worship Him in the face of adversity. Yet so many refuse to worship the Lord, simply because they don't feel like it. Like David, we need to bless the Lord at all times, and let His praises continue to be in our mouths, regardless of the circumstance.

God wants to anoint your head with fresh oil, even the

oil of joy and gladness. He wants your life to be so anointed that there's an overflow. We are blessed to be a blessing. It's time to get so full of God that there is not enough room within us to contain it. Just as God shared all of His goodness with us, He's looking for us share that goodness with others. He is El-Shaddai, the God of more than enough. This means that it is impossible to ever give away everything He has given to you.

God has planned for goodness and mercy to follow you all the days of your life. It's time to see the goodness of the Lord in every area. No matter how many mistakes you've made, no matter how many times you've sinned, God's mercy will meet your need. He will forgive you as many times as it takes. He will demonstrate His longsuffering toward you. So regardless of past experiences, God has chosen you. There's nothing you can do to change that. He will turn your mistakes into miracles and resurrect your dreams.

Wherefore seeing we also are compassed about with
so great a cloud of witnesses, let us lay aside every
weight, and the sin which doth so easily beset us
and let us run with patience the race
that is set before us.
- Hebrews 12:1 (KJV)

Today's the day to accept the call. You've been chosen to run, and the Word of God and all of heaven stand in agreement with you. There is no better time than the present.

Will you rise to the occasion and run with the full intention to win?

Printed in the United States
92120LV00006B/52-57/A